THE CITIZEN'S CHARTER

The Citizen's Charter

Edited by
J. A. CHANDLER

Dartmouth

Aldershot • Brookfield USA • Singapore • Sydney

Published by
Dartmouth Publishing Company Limited
Gower House
Croft Road
Aldershot
Hants GU11 3HR
England

Dartmouth Publishing Company
Old Post Road
Brookfield
Vermont 05036
USA

British Library Cataloguing in Publication Data
The Citizen's Charter
   1.Citizenship - Great Britain 2.Civil rights - Great
   Britain 3.Great Britain - Politics and government - 1979-
   I.Chandler, J. A., 1945-
   354.4'1

Library of Congress Cataloging-in-Publication Data
The citizen's charter / edited by J.A. Chandler.
      p.   cm.
   Includes bibliographical references and index.
   ISBN 1-85521-703-1 (hb)
   1. Administrative agencies–Great Britain–Evaluation.
  2. Executive departments–Great Britain–Evaluation.
  3. Privatization–Great Britain. 4. Government business
  enterprises–Great Britain. 5. Government productivity–Great
  Britain. 6. Citizenship–Great Britain. I. Chandler, J.A.
  JN318.C57   1996
  354.4109–dc20
                                        96-24897
                                        CIP

ISBN 1 85521 703 1
Printed in Great Britain by
Antony Rowe Ltd, Chippenham, Wiltshire

Contents

Preface   vi
Contributors   vii

1   Introduction   1
     J. A. Chandler
2   Citizen or State Consumer? A Fistful of Charters   7
     John Kingdom
3   What Price Citizenship? Public Management and the
     Citizen's Charter   24
     Howard Elcock
4   Citizens and Customer Care   40
     J. A. Chandler
5   Accountability, Openness and the Citizen's Charter   55
     Michael Hunt
6   The Citizen's Charter and Quality Management:
     Harmony or Discord?   67
     D. S. Morris and R. H. Haigh
7   The Patient's Charter   85
     Ann Wall
8   The Charter and Education   102
     Robert Leach
9   The Citizen's Charter and Housing   115
     Brian D. Jacobs
10   The Citizen's Charter and British Rail   131
     Peter Curwen
11   The Citizen's Charter in Local Government   139
     Neil Barnett and Shirley Harrison

Index   156

Preface

The Citizen's Charter has been labelled as John Major's 'big idea' and was a key element of his strategy to differentiate his leadership of the Conservative Party from that of his iron predecessor Mrs Thatcher. The initiative is more than simply window dressing but carries with it important implications for public administration and management. Norman Lewis, for example, observes in *Political Quarterly* (1993, p. 326) that:

> The changes being built upon Next Steps and flagged by the Charter are even greater in terms of size and shape of government and the underlying philosophy of governance . . . It would be foolish to underestimate Mr Major's Big Idea.

Despite its importance relatively little has been written on the initiative. This book aims to remedy this deficiency, providing an introduction to the Charter, a number of critical studies on its underlying theory and assumptions and finally studies of its application to a number of major services.

The book emerged from a Conference, 'The Waves of Change: Public Management in the 1990s' organised in 1993 by Sheffield Business School. Some of the papers in this volume were originally presented at this Conference although they have now been much revised, whilst several others have been written specifically for this book. I would like to thank all contributors who have helped to make the compilation of this volume a pleasant and rewarding task.

The technical work of ensuring a high standard of presentation has been the lot of Jenny Chambers of the Policy Research Centre, Sheffield Business School and thanks are due to her persevering work on the project. Thanks are also due to Ann Barham for accurate proof reading and compiling an excellent index. I have also received excellent help and support from editorial assistants at Dartmouth Publishing Company.

Contributors

J. A. Chandler is a senior lecturer and research fellow in the Policy Research Centre, Sheffield Business School, Sheffield Hallam University.

John Kingdom is a reader in public administration in the Sheffield Business School, Sheffield Hallam University.

Howard Elcock is professor of government in the Department of Economics and Government of the University of Northumbria.

Michael Hunt is a senior lecturer in the Policy Research Centre, Sheffield Business School, Sheffield Hallam University.

D. S. Morris is a professor of business and management in the Sheffield Business School, Sheffield Hallam University.

R. H. Haigh is a professor of business and management in the Sheffield Business School, Sheffield Hallam University.

Ann Wall is a senior lecturer in the Sheffield Business School, Sheffield Hallam University.

Robert Leach is a principal lecturer in the Faculty of Business, Leeds Metropolitan University.

Brian D. Jacobs is a reader in public administration in the Department of International Relations and Politics, Staffordshire University.

Peter Curwen is a professor of economics in the Policy Research Centre, Sheffield Business School, Sheffield Hallam University.

Neil Barnett is an ESRC management teaching fellow in the Business School, Leeds Metropolitan University.

Shirley Harrison is a senior lecturer in the Business School, Leeds Metropolitan University.

1 Introduction

J. A. CHANDLER

Citizen's Charters are now an established element in British government both at central and local levels and within the all too numerous unelected quangos. The concept has also pervaded many private sector businesses, especially those trading with the public at large, so that not a few retailers, hotels and financial agencies sport their versions of a charter.

A number of academics have seen the initiative as presaging major changes in public sector administration. As Norman Lewis observes:

> The changes being built upon Next Steps and flagged by the Charter are even greater in terms of size and shape of government and the underlying philosophy of governance. It would be foolish to underestimate Mr Major's Big Idea (Lewis, 1993, p. 326).

Despite such a view and the widespread use of the Charter concept, many commentators see the Charter movement as a rather peripheral by-product of what may be the later and less productive years of Thatcherism. Walsh (1995), for example, discusses the Charter in passing and similar recent studies on new public management do not place the initiative at centre stage but relegate the initiative largely to the level of a nodding acquaintance (Kerley, 1994; Leach et al., 1994; Zifcak, 1994).

Indifference to the idea is, perhaps, a function of its creation as John Major's 'Big Idea' designed to differentiate the hard-headed premiership of Mrs Thatcher from a regime promoting a more caring and sensitive application of the values of the New Right. The concept was readily seen by many commentators not as a substantive move to establish a new approach to the relationship between citizen and government but a means of legitimizing existing practice or worse still providing a spin doctor's gloss on the advent of a new prime minister brought forward by the Conservative Party to repair the damage to their electoral fortunes caused by the previous incumbent.

It will be suggested by the papers in this study that there is more to the concept of the Citizen's Charter than simply an electoral device. Indeed, the concept demonstrates that the Charter was largely an extension of Thatcherite values rather than a concerted attempt to move the party in a direction contrary to its chosen ideological path of the 1980s. The idea, therefore, deserves to be analysed seriously and critically as a facet of the interpretation of New Right values put into practice by governments since 1979.

The origins of the Charter

It is far from clear exactly how the Major Government latched on to the notion of the Citizen's Charter as a central device for developing the aims of the party. It was clearly not his idea in the first instance but had been put into practice by a few left-wing local authorities in order to improve local services some years before the idea became part of the Conservatives' armoury of policy initiatives. York City Council developed a Charter in 1989 initially through the initiative of its leader and chief executive, who were devising better methods of developing policies in the public interest. The authority originally conceived the idea as a contract with the public but before the publication of their ideas decided with the Magna Charta in mind, to refer to their strategy as a Charter. In 1990 a similar initiative, entitled Clarence, was established by Lothian Regional Council in Scotland to facilitate improvements in highways and lighting standards (interviews, York City Council and Lothian Regional Council).

These ideas had been sufficiently recognized by the major political parties that when the possibility of the Charter was first announced by Major as an element of a policy speech preparing the ground for the forthcoming General Election, both the Labour and Liberal Democrat parties immediately claimed that they had already put forward the idea (*The Guardian,* 25 March 1991). Shortly before the White Paper was published the Labour Party produced its own version of a Charter (*The Guardian,* 4 July 1991). The Major Charter was not, however, based on the principles developed by York City Council, which was concerned more to ensure public opinion shaped the authority's policies rather than being a customer care arrangement.

The Conservative Charter

The idea of the Citizen's Charter as a strategy to be used by the Conservative-led central government first surfaced in March 1991 and became a reality in July when, to a considerable fanfare in the press, the government published a White Paper framing the concept. The Citizen's Charter White Paper is not itself a charter but a statement of intent to secure better services to the public by giving 'the citizen a better deal through extending consumer choice and competition' (Cabinet Office, 1991). This aim is to be secured by the application of six principles, which after some rethinking came to be formulated as:

- Standards
- Information and openness
- Choice and consultation
- Courtesy and helpfulness
- Putting things right
- Value for money

As shall be seen from a number of the contributions to this study, in practice, certain of these values have been pursued more assiduously than others. For example, as Michael Hunt suggests, there has been little opening of government as a consequence of the Charter. The greatest public attention has been, instead, focused on the issue of 'standards' and 'putting things right'. The Rail Charter with its system of refunds to the public, which as Peter Curwen observes, is not normal practice for other charters, has become, in the mind of many members of the public, the most characteristic facet of the initiative.

Although the major interest in the Citizen's Charter is concentrated on the publication of standards of service provision and means of public redress if these are not attained, the charter movement as developed by the government appears to encompass a much wider and eclectic set of values.

Central to the first White Paper was the view that better standards of public service are to be achieved by schemes to privatize and contract out public services. The charters were to be seen as a means of ensuring greater efficiency in service delivery for those services that could not immediately be subject to privatization. This more general context of the Citizen's Charter is constantly referred to in the first (Cabinet Office, 1992) and second (Cabinet Office, 1994) Charter Reports, which both comment as much on the progress of privatization and contracting out as the effectiveness of the actual Charters.

Within this study the authors have, however, been largely concerned with the central innovative element of the charter initiative in setting service standards and systems for public redress. This is not, therefore, a more general survey of the progress of privatization.

The growth of the Charter

Following the announcement of the initiative the Cabinet has strenuously sought to ensure its application throughout services controlled by Whitehall (Doern, 1993). The initiative was entrusted to the Chancellor of the Duchy of Lancaster, William Waldegrave, who was responsible for the Office for Public Service and Science now simply the Office for Public Policy (OPP). A Citizen's Charter Unit was established within the office with the authority to implement the proposal. This body is principally concerned with proselytizing the initiative throughout government but needed some strong political arm twisting to secure its widespread adoption. In order to kick start the initiative John Major convened in January 1992 a seminar on the issue that included most ministers and permanent secretaries (Doern, 1993).

Most government departments have, consequently, been obliged to write charters for services with a direct impact on the public but they have also been given a fairly wide latitude as to which features of the charter principles should be applied. These departmental or, as defined by the OPP, full charters, are reviewed in draft by the Charter Unit which, after any suitable amendments, give them their seal of approval.

The enthusiasm for the initiative emanating from the Prime Minister's office has ensured that the concept has became widely established. A year after its announcement the government published in its first report on the initiative, stating that 28 Charters had been established which included the Patient's Charter and charters for the railways and benefits agencies. By 1994 the second Charter Report showed that the number of completed charters for what is indefinably termed 'main public services' had risen to 38 (Cabinet Office, 1994). At the time of writing there are 40 government departmental charters and it is anticipated that only a few more are still to be produced.

In addition to the full charters the Charter Unit has encouraged the development of the initiative throughout the public sector. Many quangos and local authorities have subsequently developed charters although these are not formally reviewed by the Citizen Charter Unit. The exact number that have been developed is not recorded but the second Charter Report listed 47 that had been developed in public agencies (Cabinet Office, 1994).

A further incentive for public agencies to establish charters was the creation of the Charter Mark award which is given to 'those who demonstrate excellence and innovation in delivering services in line with Charter principles' (Cabinet Office, 1994, p. 4). Initially 36 organizations received this accolade and by the end of 1993 a further 93 organizations had gained this award. The Mark is gained as a consequence of a reasoned application from any organization that is concerned to demonstrate how it is establishing excellence in service delivery. It is awarded for two years and is then subject to review. If an organization is subsequently found not to have lived up to its expectations the Charter Mark can be withdrawn.

The book

This study looks at both the principles that underlie the concept of Citizen's Charters and also how the idea has been applied in practice within a number of major services. The first three contributions consider the principle of the Charter in general, with particular emphasis on the concept of citizen and customer as used within the document. A further two chapters consider the Charter in relation to its concerns to secure greater quality in service delivery and ensure more open government. The remaining chapters look at the Charter from the point of view of individual service or governmental sectors. It is not, of course, possible to cover the whole range of charters and we have selected here some of the better known sectors for Charter provision such as the health service, education, housing and rail transport. The chapter on local government provides an overview of the adaption of the principle within this more independent sector of government.

The various authors of this volume have approached the concept from their own viewpoint and hence the study presents various shades of argument concerning the value of the initiative. It is intended to stimulate critical thought on the concept and to demonstrate that the charter initiative should not be lightly dismissed as an insignificant element in government strategy towards public management. As these studies indicate, the Charter has, for good or ill, been taken seriously by central government, local government and many public agencies and therefore merits some serious consideration.

References

Cabinet Office (1991), *The Citizen's Charter: Raising the Standard*, Cm 1599, HMSO, London.
Cabinet Office (1992), *The Citizen's Charter: First Report*, Cm 2101, HMSO, London.

Cabinet Office (1994), *The Citizen's Charter: Second Report*, Cm 2540, HMSO, London.

Doern, G.B. (1993), 'The UK Citizen's Charter: Origins and Implementation in Three Agencies', *Policy and Politics*, vol. 21, no. 1, pp. 17–29.

Kerley, R. (1994), *Managing Local Government*, Macmillan, London.

Leach, S., Stewart, J. and Walsh, K. (1994), *The Changing Organization and Management of Local Government*, Macmillan, London.

Lewis, N. (1993), 'The Citizen's Charter on Next Steps: A new way of governing', *Political Quarterly*, vol. 64, no. 3, pp. 316–26.

Walsh, K. (1995), *Public Services and Market Mechanisms*, Macmillan, London.

Zifcak, S. (1994), *New Managerialism*, Open University Press, Milton Keynes.

2 Citizen or State Consumer? A Fistful of Charters

JOHN KINGDOM

It might seem that John Major, in his talk of citizens and charters, has focused the attention of people on a key ethical touchstone of our age; has lifted popular debate beyond the self-interested individualism which characterized the reign of his predecessor. This chapter examines the meaning of modern citizenship and notes the difference between its formal and substantive variants. It argues that the Citizen's Charter initiative actually forms part of the broad strategy which, far from enhancing citizenship, actually undermines it. The grandiloquence of the language of citizenship and charters masks a faithful continuity with the programme broadly termed Thatcherism. The chapter concludes that professionalism and the idea of a public service ethic in the service of social rights are the more appropriate means of securing modern citizenship.

The interest in citizenship

There is a sense in which Major may be said to have caught the zeitgeist in his Citizen's Charter initiative, a genuinely 'Big Idea'. The original White Paper introducing the Citizen's Charter (Cabinet Office, 1991) was to be followed by numerous progeny in various areas of service delivery. If the Prime Minister had caught the mood of the time it was contagious, both Labour and the Liberal Democrats producing similar proposals of their own.

At a more fundamental level of debate, there has been from the 1980s a widespread revival of British journalistic and academic interest in the concept of citizenship generally (see Andrews, 1990; Heator, 1990). The idea of citizenship belongs to the unending debate about how people should live together; it is about community, the nature of membership and the relationship of the governed to the governors. This debate is not neutral and cannot be resolved by lawyers; it reflects value judgements about the purpose of society and the state.

Underlying British debate is a widespread unease about the constitution, with its vague imprecise manifestation in case law, statutes, convention and learned opinion, the absence of a Bill of Rights or Freedom of Information Act and an idiosyncratic electoral system increasingly attacked as democratically impotent.

Standards of public morality seem to be in free-fall as constitutional conventions, which once allowed people to sleep soundly in their beds, are revealed as scarcely worth the paper they would be written on. Important state functions are increasingly placed in the hands of agencies operating at an arm's length from Parliament and under the control of individuals with no acquaintance with the ballot box. Public life remains largely a male preserve. As the state is progressively privatized by government, MPs privatize themselves with cash for questions and lucrative parliamentary consultancy contracts.

Indeed, widespread allegations of corruption, secrecy and venality at the heart of government led to the instigation of the Nolan inquiry. Although its first report, appearing in May 1995, was immediately accepted in broad thrust by the Prime Minister, the Chief Whip, Richard Ryder, and Leader of the House, Tony Newton, warned darkly that many Conservative MPs would be none too happy and would oppose some of the reform proposals in a free vote later in the year. When this came on 6 November, Major had revised his position so that he now opposed disclosure of MPs' consultancy earnings but was further embarrassed to discover enough of his colleagues willing to support Labour and disclosure was carried by 291 to 266. Yet Nolan, given a three-year tenure, remains interested in turning his committee's spotlight on other dark recesses of the state, including the House of Lords, MEPs, the influence of the Freemasons on local government and the police force and, perhaps the acid test, the funding of political parties (Chittenden and Grice, 1995).

Beyond Westminster and Whitehall, there are challenges to the British centralized state from the Celtic fringes and even the English regions, while the constitutional quagmire of Northern Ireland continues as a citizenship problem *par excellence*. Political debate over police powers, gender, race and increasing poverty also raise issues of citizenship. On top of all comes the radical New Right agenda which has gone beyond a refocusing of policies to rekindle debate on the basic ideology and structure of the postwar state.

Going further, to the realm beyond the domestic sphere, there are even more fundamental citizenship issues. In Europe there is an insistent questioning posed by the development of the European Union as a new broader focus for citizenship. On a world scale the globalized news media bring into our parlours evidence of profound abuse of people and flagrant disregard for human rights. The break-up of Eastern Europe raises the debate to white heat level. Citizenship becomes a feature of national machismo and a bargaining counter in international relations.

In a changing world the concept of citizenship as traditionally understood is under considerable strain and may be outmoded, harmful and in need of revision. The concept of the sovereign nation-state around which traditional discourse largely centres is rendered fictional; all states, be they in the affluent core or at the impoverished periphery of the world economy, are locked in an embrace which may prove deadly. Economic colonization by powerful countries or private multinational corporations falsify the rights a nation might wish to confer on its people as effectively as military conquest.

Economic globalization is followed by the political as new international associations and institutions form to contain the power of private multi-nationals. Such developments are accelerated by increasingly insistent ecological crises which demand global remedies. In this precarious world system, traditional pride in national citizenship can easily shade into xenophobia and there is no moral justification for the quality of citizenship in one country being premised upon the impoverishment of another. When associated with patriotism, that last refuge of the scoundrel, citizenship can mean racism, religious and political fundamentalism and ethnic cleansing.

Athens was the crucible where citizenship was made, yet Plato declared himself a citizen not of it, but of the world. David Held declares that 'the historical moment seems to have passed for trying to define citizen's claims and entitlements in terms of a national community' (Held, 1991, p. 24). Perhaps the most insistent moral call today must be for a body of human rights to accrue to each individual regardless of formal citizenship claims (Bottomore, 1992, pp. 85–92).

Hence the opening suggestion that Major, in his talk of citizens and charters, has focused the attention of people on a key ethical touchstone of our age. He has lifted popular ethical debate above the individualistic self-interest which characterized the reign of his predecessor. Or has he? We can begin to address this question with a brief consideration of the two central concepts: the charter and citizenship.

Citizenship

Citizenship implies status within society and may be contrasted with the term 'subject', which implies an absence of status: subservience to a monarch. Hence both American and French revolutions asserted citizenship as an essential cornerstone of human dignity.

Traditional citizenship

This debate has continued from the times of the ancient Greeks, through Cicero and the Roman Republics, the thirteenth-century Italian city states and Calvin's Geneva to the English Commonwealth. For the ancient Greeks, membership of the city state was akin to that of a family, entailing a twinning of rights of participation and duties. Aristotle defined citizens as all those sharing in the civic process of 'ruling and being ruled in turn' (1946, p. 134). The purpose of citizenship to the Greeks was to attain the good life: the civilized life. It is from the Romans that we get the more legalistic idea of guaranteed individual rights (Sabine, 1963, p. 65). The reciprocity between rights and duties is a logical necessity; the duties of one protect the rights of another. From this it is clear that, although conferring rights and duties upon individuals, citizenship is necessarily a collectivist concept; it 'propels us towards the idea of transcendence, a greater collectivity in which we get beyond our local identities and concerns' (Phillips, 1991, p. 81).

Yet traditional citizenship can be problematic. In the first place it is not necessarily egalitarian in effect. It can be an exclusive as well as an inclusive device. While the rights of all citizens may be equal, all residents of a state or community may not be citizens. In the Greek city states citizens were outnumbered by slaves, women and aliens. Under feudalism the civilized life was the preserve of an aristocratic elite. Jews in Nazi Germany, black people in apartheid South Africa, and guest-workers in Germany today are further testimony to the excluding potential of the concept. In almost all cultures and throughout history women have been subjugated through the instrument of citizenship. Citizenship has also been tied to class and property. Indeed, much history can be portrayed in terms of the struggle against the exclusive nature of citizenship.

Neither was traditional citizenship necessarily democratic. The Greek city states permitted differing levels of participation in government, restricting variously the quality of active citizenship. In some states it meant no more than a right to attend city meetings, while in others it entailed eligibility for public office. Hence citizenship, in practice, can be an instrument of oppression. If it is to manifest the ethical ideals claimed for it, it must be universal, according status rights and duties equally upon all. However, the problems do not end with legal universality. Though a necessary condition, this is not a sufficient one. It is important to distinguish between formal and substantive citizenship.

Formal and substantive citizenship

This raises a problem which is all the greater for being hidden. Formal citizenship may entail nothing more than acknowledgement of membership of a nation-state; international law adopts this view, making no distinction between citizenship and nationality. Yet only if citizenship confers a capacity to participate fully in political, economic and social life, on an equal basis with all others, can it be regarded as substantive. Formal citizenship does not necessarily realize substantive citizenship and substantive citizenship can be eroded while formal citizenship remains intact. The distinction is of crucial significance in considering the meaning of citizenship in the modern world. A person unable to act as a full member of the community might just as well be designated an alien or a slave, as in the Greek city state.

Modern citizenship

It is clear that many of the strains of citizenship running throughout history would not satisfy modern expectations of substantive citizenship. In a seminal essay of 1950, T. H. Marshall produced what can be regarded as a classic statement of modern citizenship (Marshall, 1992).

This comprised three kinds of rights: civil (to life and limb, recourse to the law through a fair trial in the courts, own property, buy and sell, retain the products of one's labour, make contracts); political (to vote, speak one's opinions, make political speeches, join unions, form political associations, stand for parliament, even form a government) and social (to enjoy an acceptable standard of economic welfare and security through housing, education, income and health). Marshall portrayed the development of modern citizenship in Britain beginning in the eighteenth century, as a gradual extension of these rights from a narrow aristocratic elite to an ever-widening constituency.

Yet there was a paradox in that the extension of citizenship, with its implications of equality, took place alongside the growth of capitalism, with its contrary implication of inequality. The contradiction had been noted by Marx, who saw the modern individual driven by two conflicting identities: the *bourgeois* and the citizen. How could two opposing principles appear to flourish side by side? Marshall found the answer in the fact that the development was evolutionary in nature. It was possible to assign the formative period of each group of rights to a different century, 'civil rights to the eighteenth, political to the nineteenth and social to the twentieth' (Marshall, 1992, p. 10).

Hence the core of citizenship which emerged during the early stages of capitalism comprised civil rights. These were not concessions to a competitive market economy; by breaking old feudal ties they were crucially necessary to its success. People gained the rights to acquire and protect possession of material things, but possession in itself was not a right. Indeed, the extension of civil rights made possible resistance to state social policy on the grounds that sufficient means for self-protection were already available. This limited view of citizenship was supported by the dominant thinking of the classical political economists (embodied in the 1834 Poor Law reforms), which saw state assistance for the victims of the capitalist system as damaging to the economy and, indeed, to the human species.

Individuals were to use their civil rights to secure their needs for food and shelter and so on. The equality bestowed by citizenship was an equal right to compete. Insofar as there was state or private welfare it was charity; not a right of citizenship, but an alternative to it. Paupers forfeited liberty by entering the workhouse and were automatically disenfranchised. Similarly, the protection offered by the Factory Acts was directed at other disenfranchised categories, women and children, who were not considered citizens at all (Marshall, 1992, p. 15).

By the same token, the extending political rights of the nineteenth century remained effectively a class preserve of the *bourgeoisie*, with various devices (anti-union legislation, property qualification for voters, electoral deposits) inhibiting effective working class participation.

In reality, class prejudice and economic inequality meant that substantive citizenship was beyond the reach of the mass of ordinary people. There was no apparent conflict between the development of citizenship and the growth of capitalism because the citizenship on offer was, for most people, not of the substantive kind. The conflict between capitalism and citizenship only becomes real when the latter is both universal and substantive. This only occurs when social rights (to health, education, shelter and economic security) are added to the mix.

These are not merely final strands enhancing the richness of a tapestry of citizenry, they constitute the peculiar essence of modern citizenship, being different in kind from civil rights. They reflect the fundamental distinction between liberal democracy and social democracy. Civil rights belong to the liberal state which claims not to create rights but to preserve those held to be antecedent to it: natural rights. To be substantive, citizenship under capitalism must entail rights created by the state. Therefore social rights represent the most sophisticated and advanced element of modern citizenship. Moreover, it is the social rights that generate most overtly the duties associated with citizenship. Thus, for example, paying tax is a duty of citizenship, but in the liberal state it is an unfortunate cost.

Hence, the postwar social democratic settlement presented the most advanced form of citizenship achieved in Britain. The electoral landslide of the Labour Party, and the acceptance of the new agenda by the Conservatives, appeared to mark a fundamental culture shift in the body politic. The contradiction between citizenship and capitalism, which in the eighteenth and nineteenth centuries had been obscured by effectively denying substantive citizenship, appeared to have been resolved by the emergence of a new form of capitalism.

The capitalism detailed by Marx and Engels had been replaced by a modern form of diffused ownership through share holdings. The new leaders of industry were salaried managers with no interest in grinding down their workforces. In the new order it was recognized that social rights could actually be functional for the economy by relieving it of much social responsibility and legitimating the idea of profit. The left's critique of the postwar settlement maintained that continuing social inequality meant that, in practice, many rights still existed only in the formal sense. Yet this was a harsh judgement; with common rights to housing, health, education, economic security and employment, citizenship was certainly more substantive than before.

No charters please, we're British

Charters are documents conferring powers, rights, duties and privileges. They can be granted willingly by enlightened rulers or wrested from despots through revolution. In the real world their use has been closely identified with the growth of citizenship. They enjoy a noble place in the advance of western civilization; a tool of those who would assail the towers of elitism. In the

Magna Charta the barons claimed rights from the monarch. In 1683 the first enactment of the first assembly of New York Colony, though disallowed by the English Parliament, was a Charter of Liberties and Privileges. In France the petitioners of 1789 listed their grievances in the form of a charter. The nineteenth-century English Chartists presented their 'People's Charter', which detailed their claims for rights and democracy. In contemporary times the UN Charter sets out in its seventy Articles principles for peace, human rights, justice and international cooperation. The Czech 'Charter 77' movement inspired libertarians, and found an echo in our own 'Charter 88' which, in addition, recalls the 'Glorious Revolution' of 1688.

However, as a written and tangible guarantee of rights, a charter has been unwelcome in a political culture that has for long venerated vague conventions more than statutes, has created no entrenched law, has regarded the fact that its constitution is unwritten as something to boast about and has displayed a cavalier disregard for the notion of a Bill of Rights. Though willing to ratify the European Convention on Human Rights in 1951, the British government fought shy of enacting it into domestic law. Today British citizens are in the anomalous position of being unable to use the convention as a basis for approaching their own courts though, rather clumsily, they can use it to appeal to the European Court on Human Rights once they have exhausted the domestic avenues. While other states fashion Freedom of Information Acts, Britain promulgates Official Secrets Acts, by which means its populace is kept in greater ignorance of the doings of its rulers than any other in the developed world.

The British government says '*Non*' to the social chapter of the Maastricht Treaty (claiming 'game, set and match' for so doing), 'No' to a Freedom of Information Bill, 'No' to a written constitution and turns a deaf ear to a panoply of constitutional safeguards demanded by Charter 88. With their ancient monarchy preserved in aspic, the British are constantly reminded that, in the eyes of the constitution, they remain subjects rather than citizens. The culture is one of deference where people are granted tenuous privileges rather than inalienable rights.

It can be compellingly argued that no contemporary citizenry appears in greater need of a charter than the British. Perhaps Major can indeed claim to have found his moment in history. Can such a claim be justified? In order to understand the Citizen's Charter initiative we must examine what has been happening to citizenship during the New Right era.

Citizenship under the New Right – Honey I shrunk the public domain

The New Right thinking is essentially individualistic. Its theoretical under-pinnings come from classical liberalism, utilitarianism, neoclassical economics and public choice theory: schools of thought employing a logico-deductive method premised upon the isolated, self-seeking individual. Substantive modern citizenship, with social and political as well as civil elements, could not be expected to fit comfortably within this logical universe. So proved the case. The Thatcher years saw an erosion of both political and social rights and a reduction in the duties associated with them. This was no unintended consequence of other policies but a central declared aim. To Thatcher it was a mission to kill what she referred to as 'socialism'. The lessening of the duties of citizenship was pre-eminently to be achieved through reductions in income taxes (though of course total tax yield rose throughout the period). How were political, social and civil rights affected?

Political rights These were assailed variously. A legislative fusillade reduced trade union powers in various ways. Indeed, for Thatcher, trade unionists in general could hardly be seen as citizens at all; dubbed the 'enemy within', they were as effectively vanquished as the foreign enemy in the South Atlantic. There was even an attempt to reduce the funds available to the main opposition party. Privatization reduced the range of activities under democratic control as citizens were replaced by shareholders. Elected local government was another principal target. Some services were passed onto the private sector, others, including urban development, to a menagerie of newly created quangos. Appointment by political patronage was enlarged at the expense of electoral representation; many new local quangos were placed in the hands of appointees largely from the business community. In the NHS, opting-out removed hospitals and community care units from health authority control and elected councillors were replaced on health authorities, again by non-elected appointees.

Of deep significance, a major convention of government – consultation with interests – was curtailed. Under the name of pluralism this had been seen as one of the principal factors mitigating a creaking and idiosyncratic electoral system. The electoral system itself was revealed more obviously as a restraint upon, rather than a source of, political rights as Liberal Democrat voters suffered from a disproportionality of representation. The political right of freedom of speech was threatened as the BBC came under demoralizing bombardment, its director general unceremoniously dispatched in favour of a placeperson.

Social rights   These were eroded directly by means of an extensive programme of cuts in the welfare state affecting housing, education, health care and social services. Hence, the decade saw an increase in inequality induced by fiscal policies and unemployment. Abolition of wages councils removed protection against low wages. The idea that modern citizenship entailed a right to work was challenged by the repudiation of Keynes and all his works, the government insisting that only private sector initiative could create jobs. The topic of a new underclass became common in journalistic and academic analysis.

In place of social rights Thatcher often spoke of other values: patriotism, family values, self-help, choice and voluntarism. Yet these are not citizenship values: patriotism can mean racism; the family can be a fortress against society and a prison for many women; self-help replaces duty to others with duty to the self; choice tends to mean selection from the shelves of the supermarket on the basis of wallet size; while voluntarism can expose the weak to the cold hand of charity, replacing the duty to give with judgemental paternalism and substituting cap-doffing humility for rights.

Civil rights   However, although the strategy eroded political and social rights it left civil rights, the necessary underpinning for the capitalist economy, largely unscathed. Indeed, the forces of law and order were strengthened in order to protect them better. Hence, the rhetoric was able to tell of rolling back the state rather than rolling back citizenship. Of course the erosion of political and social rights necessarily limited the ability of people to use civil rights, a consequence made more acute by limitations on the legal aid system.

In other words, a different view of citizenship was being promulgated. It is not surprising that Thatcher frequently spoke with atavistic longing of the nineteenth century, a time when citizenship was, for most people, formal rather than substantive.

Hence, the replacement of Thatcher by Major becomes extremely important to the citizenship debate. Although it might seem no small irony that a government with a project systematically to weaken substantive citizenship should begin to talk the grandiose language of citizenship and charters, the mood was for change. The Citizen's Charter was soon heralded as Major's 'big idea'. The choice of the term itself could be taken as an implicit recognition that citizenship was in jeopardy. The initiative could be seen as signalling a symbolic break with the immediate past. This is the question to consider.

A Citizen's Charter – change or continuity?

Closer examination suggests the disjuncture is largely illusory. Whether or not Major would wish to distance himself from the stylistic aspects of Thatcherism, his initiative is entirely within the framework of the New Right thinking which marked the 1980s. Behind the rhetoric it maintains the broad hegemonic project of Thatcher, the policy trajectory of her government and the neoliberal anti-statism which marked her relationship with public bureaucracy.

Continuing the hegemonic project – the politics of legitimation

For most people the idea of being able to complain, and claim recompense for poor service, if not a particularly '*big* idea', is still not a *bad* idea. However, in terms of a political strategy from the right it has deeper significance. The initiative can be explained in terms of the way people think about politics and power, the idea of hegemony in the Gramscian sense, legitimation; the politics of the mind. For several scholars a key element of Thatcherism was a 'hegemonic project' in which popular ideological perceptions accepted the right-wing programme as a common sense solution to social problems (Hall, 1980).

O'Connor's (1973) thesis that the existence of a welfare state (which many have seen as the saviour of modern capitalism) cannot ultimately avert crisis sets the scene. As state welfare increases, the tax revenue required will undermine the very profitability it is designed to secure. The resulting 'fiscal crisis of the state' illustrates the paradox that, although the system cannot exist without a welfare state, neither can it exist with it.

One response to this may be expected to take the form of cuts in state social expenditure. This is the erosion of social rights which we have already characterized as an erosion of substantive citizenship. This enterprise poses new dangers; as the British know from the problem of Northern Ireland, the contraction of substantive citizenship for sections of a population promises a threat to social stability. Hence, a policy of this kind must be attended by a psychological project in which either people can be brought to accept their loss willingly as a necessary price to pay for some greater good, or the loss can be obscured with counter rhetoric.

Such legitimation was very apparent during the assault on the state. The proclaimed 'conviction' of Thatcher spoke to many ordinary folk, and the apparently moral dimensions of her project led some to believe her to have wrested the moral high ground from the left, making the Conservatives almost unrecognizable as a thinking party. The message entailed much elaboration of the virtues of the free market, an argument that public sector management was intrinsically inefficient and a general deprecation of public sector bureaucrats and professionals. At the same time, terms such as 'dependency culture', 'postwar funk' and 'scrounger' were employed to debase the currency of modern social democratic citizenship. Thatcher's popularity and electoral success confirmed that popular culture responded to the message. Her style was aptly characterized as 'authoritarian populism' (Hall, 1980).

However, the manner of Thatcher's departure from office suggested that this particular legitimation strategy was losing its effectiveness. With the shimmer of the Falklands victory dimming, the 1980s boom but a memory, and unemployment rising, people were no longer experiencing the 'feel good factor'. The loss of substantive citizenship was becoming more apparent. A new style was required for the legitimation strategy and the mission to deliver it fell upon Major.

The new leader seemed to recognize this need for change. Much of his rhetoric, in contrast to the confrontational 'enemy within' talk of Thatcher, was to be of a one-nation kind. The emollient tone spoke of restoring 'active citizenship', of a nation 'at peace with itself', of a 'classless society' and of ladies cycling to church without fear of molestation. However, this was still a legitimation strategy for a New Right programme. Substantive policy in areas such as the free market, privatization, public sector managerialism, NHS reform, educational centralism, the enlargement of the non-elective state and so on, remained largely unchanged.

Continuing the policy trajectory – the politics of illusion

How can the Citizen's Charter initiative fit snugly within the general policy environment outlined above, which so reduced the scope of modern substantive citizenship during the Thatcher reign? It can do so because the key words are used rather in the manner employed by Humpty Dumpty, to mean 'just what I please'. In reality, the Citizen's Charters are not charters in any real sense, neither are they about true and substantive citizenship.

When is a charter not a charter? The Major charters are of a quite different genus to the noble declarations which have underscored the march of civilization. They are not petitioned from below but conferred from above. The position of the apostrophe reveals that they succour the individual rather than the collectivity.

They find their home not in the fight for the Rights of Man but in the commercial world of 'money back if not absolutely delighted' guarantees and 'have a nice day' service. They do not confer rights upon citizens *per se*, but upon subjects seen as state customers. They place stress on individual self-help, competition, and redress through penalties and fines. As befits a nation of shopkeepers, the state becomes a great retail complex.

Seen in this way there is clearly no break with the policy traditions of Thatcherism. Indeed, well before talk of Citizen's Charters, the marketization of the public sector had seen passengers, subscribers, borrowers, patients, tenants, parents, students and so on eerily transmogrified into customers. Even the Inland Revenue called its clients customers. The citizen becomes an atomized shopper armed with a fistful of charters.

Yet the designation charter is political hyperbole of an extravagant kind. People may feel empowered (though this is debatable), but they are not empowered as citizens.

When is a citizen not a citizen? Like that of the charter, the concept of citizenship is subject to serious debasement: a collectivist idea, status through membership of society, is redefined in individualistic, contractual terms. The public is seen as buying services, through payment of taxes, and increasingly other charges, rather than acquiring rights through community membership (Stewart and Walsh, 1992, p. 507). The justification for such a relationship between people comes from liberal individualism rather than civic republicanism (Oldfield, 1990). It offers an illusion of citizenship and is in no sense a departure from the Thatcher mission to atomize through the avowal that 'there is no such thing as society'.

It is an illusion because, as Edgar Wilson argues: 'It is perverse and futile . . . to impose financial penalties for delays to services which are delayed in the first place because of lack of finance' (1992, p. xiii). If policies cannot be influenced at source there can be no pretence of citizenship.

Continuing the anti-statism

The Citizen's Charter initiative is most clearly at one with the Thatcher project in its anti-statism. It is a continuing problem for the libertarian left that the development of social rights can be associated with a sense of alienation as individuals confront large organizations. Distrust and fear of faceless bureaucracy is deeply ingrained in liberal thought. From Locke, through the recondite works of Weber to the evocative novels of Orwell, Kafka and Koestler, the institutions of the state feature as oppressors rather than liberators. Moreover, the public choice theory which informed the thinking of right-wing think tanks contained a sustained critique of public bureaucracy on the grounds that state employees must be empire-builders whose self-interested aspirations lead to a profligate 'oversupply' of their services, escalating taxation, high-handed paternalism and public waste, while actually harming the interests of those they exist to serve (Niskanen, 1973). Although even a social democratic haven like Sweden experienced the problem (Ryden and Bergstrom, 1982), it was the ominous presence of the party-machine bureaucracies of Eastern Europe that Thatcher evoked in her anti-socialist rhetoric.

Hence, although political fear of bureaucracy was for long more apparent from the left than the right (commentators such as Laski, Benn and Crowther-Hunt doubting the ability of an elitist civil service to implement a programme of social democracy), it was from the New Right that the serious assaults came. For Thatcher, the civil service displayed a dangerously pinkish hue, 'its assumptions . . . corrosively infected by social democracy' (Young, 1989, p. 153). The Thatcher agenda thus entailed a sustained assault on public sector bureaucrats and the professionals.

Again it is clear that the idea of the Citizen's Charter, a whip with which to flagellate *homo bureaucraticus*, is entirely in keeping with the Thatcherite strategy. It works on the principle of threat and punishment of an intrinsic evil: the state. It offers a government embarrassed by shortcomings in state services another advantage: scapegoating. It promises to increase the uncertainty and demoralization of state employees which was a characteristic of Thatcherism. It is a repudiation of the idea of a public service ethic, professionalism and trust.

Must there be darkness at noon?

Professionalism and trust

It would be wrong to dismiss the problems the social democratic state can pose for liberty. Certainly writers on the left in Britain have decried the paternalism embedded in the welfare state which could remove autonomy and dignity from recipients.

However, while it is eminently desirable that trains and doctors run to time, that motorways are not littered with cones and that benefits agency employees be polite, individualist consumerism cannot be the answer. In a world becoming increasingly technical and complex, the customer does not always know best. Trust becomes an essential feature of life in modern society (Giddens, 1990, pp. 79–112). We must perforce rely upon the professionalism of experts, be they motor mechanics, computer programmers, educationalists or brain surgeons.

Trust can only be rationally exercised if it is twinned with the idea of professionalism. Professionalism entails an occupational group accepting a duty to perform in the interests of those receiving their service, even where this might conflict with personal self-interest. The archetype of this ethic is the Hippocratic oath of the medical profession. Although the reality of the collective behaviour of professionals may actually be portrayed as a threat to society (Illich, 1977), there is no alternative other than an entirely unrealistic retreat into a pre-industrial order. Modern society must be based on trust rather than threat, on cooperation rather than competition. We cannot expect better education because we are able to harass and beat our teachers; doctors will not wield their scalpels more dextrously if they operate beneath a hanging sword of Damocles.

The ubiquity of trust was shown in the paradox that, while the New Right sought to denigrate and demoralize the professions, people were asked to trust in various ways: to place faith in toxic waste disposal experts; in non-elected appointees to state positions; in managers as opposed to professionals; in nuclear power stations. They were also to trust the decisions of politicians to privatize this and that, to define the school curriculum, and dispatch them to war in the South Atlantic and the Gulf. They were even told to trust that the NHS would be 'safe with us'. Most of all they were to trust the hidden hand which guides the market.

Professional ethics and trust are concepts embedded in the idea of modern citizenship. The answer to the question of securing the good state must lie not in entrusting it to the profit-seeking ethic of the private sector or in the transmogrification of citizens into customers. It must come at a more fundamental level in the heightened sense of the ethic of community, professionalism and public service.

This can only come through a revival of true substantive citizenship. Marshall had been well aware of the crucial difference between citizens and customers. The former's expectations are not claims to be met in each individual case when presented: 'The obligation of the state is towards society as a whole, whose remedy in case of default lies in parliament or a local council, instead of to individual citizens' (Marshall, 1992, p. 35).

The state must provide mechanisms for 'explicitly political activity, in which people who are equals address collective and general concerns' (Phillips, 1991, p. 82). A public realm must be cultivated promoting values of openness, accountability, responsibility, a belief in a public good which is distinct from the sum of individual goods, an ethic of public service, respect for professionalism within the public sector and machinery for participation at various levels of the state.

References

Andrews, G. (ed.) (1991), *Citizenship*, Lawrence and Wishart, London.

Aristotle (1946) *Politics* (ed. Barker, E.), Clarendon Press, Oxford.

Bottomore, T. (1992), 'Citizenship and Social Class, Forty Years on', in Marshall, T.H. and Bottomore, T., *Citizenship and Social Class*, Pluto Press, London.

Cabinet Office (1991), *The Citizen's Charter: Raising the Standard*, Cm 1599, HMSO, London.

Chittenden, M. and Grice, A. (1995), 'The New Gravy Train', *The Sunday Times*, 14 May.

Elshtain, J. B. (1981), *Public Man, Private Woman*, Princeton University Press, Princeton.

Giddens, A. (1990) *The Consequences of Modernity*, Polity Press, Oxford.

Hall, S. (1980), 'Popular Democratic Versus Authoritarian Populism', in Hunt, A. (ed.), *Marxism and Democracy*, Lawrence and Wishart, London.

Hall, S. and Held, D. (1989), 'Citizens and Citizenship', in Hall, S. and Jacques, M. (eds), *New Times*, Lawrence and Wishart, London, pp. 173–88.

Heator, D. (1990), *Citizenship*, Longman, Harlow.

Held, D. (1991), 'Between State and Civil Society', in Andrews, G. (ed.), *Citizenship*, Lawrence and Wishart, London, pp. 19–25.

Ignatieff, M. (1991), 'Citizenship and Moral Narcissism', in Andrews, G. (ed.), *Citizenship*, Lawrence and Wishart, London, pp. 26–36.

Illich, I. (1977), *Limits to Medicine*, Penguin, Harmondsworth.

Marshall, T. H. (1992), 'Citizenship and Social Class', reprinted in Marshall, T. H. and Bottomore, T., *Citizenship and Social Class*, Pluto, London (first published, 1950).

Marshall, T. H. and Bottomore T. (1992), *Citizenship and Social Class*, Pluto Press, London.

Niskanen, W. A. (1973), *Bureaucracy: Servant or Master?*, Institute of Economic Affairs, London.

Oldfield, A. (1990), *Citizenship and Community: Civic Republicanism in the Modern World*, Routledge, London.

O'Connor, J. (1973), *The Fiscal Crisis of the State*, St Martin's Press, New York.

Phillips, A. (1991), 'Citizenship and Feminist Theory', in Andrews, G. (ed.), *Citizenship*, Lawrence and Wishart, London, pp. 76–88.

Ryden, B. and Bergstrom, V. (eds) (1982), *Sweden: Choices for Economic and Social Policy in the 1980s*, Allen and Unwin, London.

Sabine, G. (1963), *A History of Political Theory*, Harrap, London (3rd edn).

Schumpeter, J. A. (1942*), Capitalism, Socialism and Democracy*, Allen and Unwin, London (6th edn).

Stewart, J. and Walsh, K. (1992), 'Management of Public Services', *Public Administration*, no. 70 (Winter 1992), pp. 499–518.

Wilson E. (1992), *A Very British Miracle*, Pluto Press, London.

Young, H. (1989), *One of Us*, Macmillan, London.

3 What Price Citizenship? Public Management and the Citizen's Charter

HOWARD ELCOCK

Introduction

This essay is not an attempt to belittle the Citizen's Charter. Even less is it a complaint about a measure which has strengthened the citizen's rights to decent treatment by and redress against the state, at least to some extent, under a constitution in which citizens' rights are both weakly articulated and incompletely protected (see, for example, Street, 1963; Stacey, 1975; Hewitt, 1982; Taylor, 1992). However, it is an attempt to improve both the quality of the debate about and the implementation of the Charter itself, by clarifying the language that is being used in and around it.

Some of the words most frequently used in the continuing debate about how to develop the management of public service organizations are used loosely, with little apparent thought being given to their precise meaning (see Elcock, 1995). For instance, in his initial announcement of the Citizen's Charter, the Prime Minister wrote of government services that:

> Where there is no choice and a citizen cannot go elsewhere when [public] services fall below standard, it is more, not less important that the standard of service is high. Those who provide public services therefore have a special duty to respond to the needs of their customers and clients (Prime Minister's announcement of 22 July 1991).

One can only agree with the general sentiment expressed here. However, in John Major's statement, the terms 'citizen', 'customer' and 'client' were used interchangeably. The problem this poses is that it confuses some central concepts concerning the relationship between the individual person and servants of the state, as well as those between individuals collectively and the state as a corporate organization – or set of corporate organizations – which in turn obscures the issues concerning what the relationships should be. This is not merely a linguistic quibble; it is an issue that goes to the heart of what the relationship between state and citizen in a democracy should be.

The Citizen's Charter specifies four aims:

- *Quality* – A sustained new programme for improving the quality of public services – [but quality is not defined in the Charter].
- *Choice* – Choice wherever possible between competing providers is the best spur to quality improvement. [One has to ask whether competition is the only or even the best spur to better service available. Open access to customers coupled with responsiveness to their comments may be just as good a spur to good performance].
- *Standards* – The citizen must be told what service standards are and to be able to act where service is unacceptable.
- *Value* – The citizen is also a tax-payer; public services must give value for money within a tax bill the nation can afford (Cabinet Office, 1991, p. 4).

These aims are indeed desirable from the point of view of the customers, clients or consumers of public services. What is less immediately self-evident is that together they constitute the rights, expectations and obligations of a citizen.

This is especially the case in those many areas where the citizen has no choice but to use the services provided by the state. This occurs in various contexts. The first is non-excludable public goods, such as defence or the maintenance of public order, where all members of the community must contribute but no one individual gains a specific benefit. The benefits accrue to all the members of a safe and orderly society. Second comes the case of collective goods, such as clean air, where the state intervenes to secure a collective benefit. The third is where the state is the only possible provider, as with the National Insurance system, where the state collects insurance contributions and distributes them to claimants when they need them, for instance when they become unemployed or ill. It is also the case when he or she may have to use state services unwillingly because he or she is subjected to social control by the state, for instance when arrested by the police on suspicion of having committed an offence against the law. In all these cases, the aims proposed would be appropriate when citizens are more nearly customers, because they then have a choice whether to accept the service or not, as well as from whom they wish to receive it. However, they are more or less inappropriate where these conditions do not apply. The aims of the

Citizen's Charter constitute a worthy but limited range of objectives, which are coloured by an ideological bias in favour of the private sector ethos and the economics of the free market. The assumption is above all that competition among rival suppliers of public services is the best – perhaps the only – way to secure efficient services which meet their customers' needs.

It must be added that many observers have detected in the Thatcher era a concerted effort to reduce citizens' participation in government decision-making, except through market mechanisms. This can be seen in the concerted attack mounted by successive governments since 1979 on local government (Jones and Stewart, 1984; Elcock, 1986). It can also be seen in the changes in the town and country planning system which strengthen the power of developers relative to that of politicians and local residents (Thornley, 1990) as well as in the government's unwillingness to heed the views of local police authorities (Savage, 1990). In so far as any new form of participation has developed, it is through market research exercises designed to test people's awareness of public services, the extent to which they use them and the valuation they place on them (Fenwick and Harrop, 1988). However, apart from any other limitations on such methods, participation is then confined to those members of the public who are selected to be respondents within the sample survey.

The distinctions both between various roles, such as those of citizen and customer and in the nature of their contacts with the state, are also important where charters aim to give guarantees of the position of particular groups within the polity. Examples include National Insurance contributors (A Contributor's Charter), employers (An Employers' Charter) or persons looking for work and claiming unemployment benefit (The Job-Seeker's Charter). The latter three charters are concerned chiefly with ensuring the provision of speedy, sympathetic and polite service for the groups of people with whom the relevant government organizations (the contributions, benefits and employment service agencies) have to relate. As such, their concern is with relationships with individuals as clients or customers rather than citizens. Derek Heater (1992) makes this point by inquiring of the Citizen's Charter:

> But does it really concern citizenship? The Charter relates to the individual *qua* economic being, operating in a society driven by market forces, not *qua* political being, participating (however tangentially) in the processes of government (Heater, 1992, p. 440).

This is the nub of the issue addressed here. To meet the aims of the Citizen's Charter entails changing the organizational cultures of many public services, away from 'bureaucratic paternalism' (Hoggett and Hambleton, 1987) and towards responsiveness to consumers. Robin Hambleton (1992) argues that where the state has been largely dismantled and replaced by private contractors, people are treated as customers, whereas where the public sector remains dominant or at least a public service ethos is maintained, as would be the case in his decentralized and empowering states, people are treated as both customers and citizens. Again, however, this presents an incomplete, if more sophisticated, picture of what is required of services provided for citizens (see Lovell, 1992).

Some clarification is therefore required of the language being used to discuss citizenship, not only in the interest of linguistic accuracy but also because the status of a citizen is different from that of a customer. It confers a different set of rights, duties and obligations both on the citizen, customer or client, as well as on the public servants who must deal with their needs, wants and purposes. This relationship is also of central importance to the management of public services because the framework of rights and duties within which individuals' and social groups' relationships with the state are conducted are necessarily different from those which govern the relationship between manufacturers or retailers and their customers (Elcock, 1991, pp. 37–8). The structures of accountability and control that define these relationships in government are very different from those in the private or market sector, as are the nature and range of the goals that governments must seek to achieve.

In order to further this discussion, we must seek some definitions of the various terms used in the Citizen's Charter debate, as well as in the wider debate about the nature of modern public management of which it forms part. Definitions of the roles of citizen, subject, customer, client and consumer are needed in order both to enable debate about relationships between government and people to proceed, as well as to seek the most appropriate ways to manage and improve those relationships. To assist in this process of clarification, we shall use the terms developed in W. N. Hohfeld's treatment of rights and duties (1919), in which he defined both a set of legal correlatives and a set of legal opposites. Thus the existence of a right carries with it both a correlative duty imposed both on the citizen and others to honour it, as well as a prohibition against interference with the exercise of the right – in Hohfeld's terminology a 'no-right' because it will often be expressed in the phrase 'You have no right to . . .'. Citizens may also enjoy privileges, powers and immunities which bring with them their own correlatives and opposites.

These concepts can assist us in clarifying the issues raised by the Citizen's Charter and the debate about public management. Hohfeld's relationships do not work perfectly in this context but by applying them to the definition of the terms being used in the Citizen's Charter debate they may assist us in examining the definitional issues involved. Their use also has the virtue of recognizing that these legal terms define collective relationships: the state is a collectivity and individuals must recognize collective as well as individual relationships with it.

Defining the terms of the Charter

A *citizen* has the right to participate in the government of his or her community: Aristotle defined citizenship in terms of the citizen's

> . . . *participation* in judgement and authority, that is, holding office, legal, political, administrative . . . they have the power and it would be ridiculous to deny their participation in authority (Artistotle, 1962, Book III, Chapter 1, pp. 102–3, emphasis added).

Citizens have a correlative *duty* to participate – for example, they have a moral duty to use their votes and a legal duty to undertake jury service. Hence they have collective obligations to their community. David Held (1992) has likewise argued that citizenship entails participation, either directly in the affairs of the community or through taking part in a competition for control over the state and its resources. This again entails taking heed of the collective needs and interests of their community, as well as the citizen's individual desires and needs (Gyford, 1991). Somewhat more vaguely, several leading government ministers have talked in recent years about the need to develop the 'active citizen' – a citizen who takes an active part in community affairs (see Gyford, 1991). The citizen's government also has the corresponding duties to permit free participation in the making of collective decisions and to take account of the views expressed by citizens exercising those rights and privileges.

Citizens have basic rights with which the government has no right to interfere, except where the security of the community is immediately affected. The 'Clear and Present Danger' and the 'Clear and Probable

Danger' tests were defined by the United States Supreme Court when it sought to determine whether or not the federal government was entitled to abridge basic freedoms in order to protect the Constitution from the possibility of overthrow by the American Communist Party. The Court took different views in successive cases as to how imminent the threat had to be to justify the abridgement of the right to freedom of speech (*Dennis v. United States*, 1949; *Yates v. United States*, 1951; see McCloskey, 1960). These rights protect the citizenry's ability to debate what goals the state is seeking to achieve, make demands upon it and criticize its performance in relation to their own individual and collective needs and desires. They should also be enforceable in the courts: Sir Kenneth Stowe (1992) has argued that a good Citizen's Charter is one that 'is in every respect justiciable, i.e. open to redress in the High Court. Surely this is a reasonable test to apply' (1992, p. 389; see also Taylor, 1992). There is hence an essential form of accountability downwards from state to citizens through the courts and other redress procedures, as well as the accountability upwards of public servants to the elected representatives who are chosen in representative liberal democracies to give expression to the wishes of the citizenry (Mill, 1972; Held, 1992).

Subjects have duties, above all a duty to obey the state, which has the corresponding right to instruct them and to expect that its instructions will be obeyed. Subjects do not participate in the taking of collective decisions but they may have some immunities with which the state has no right to interfere, except to prevent immediate threats to its safety. Otherwise, in Aristotle's terms the government 'rest(s) on force and disregard(s) the common weal' (1962, Book III, Chapter 3). Such a state would in Aristotle's terms be a tyranny. It would be, however, the only acceptable form of state if one accepts Thomas Hobbes's view that the only way to avoid the war of all against all is for all members of society to surrender their rights to Leviathan in order that the state may keep order among individuals who will otherwise go to war with one another. For Hobbes, the only right that an individual cannot thus surrender to the state is his or her right of self-defence, so prisoners have to be forcibly led to prison or the gallows (Hobbes, 1968). The concept of the subject is relevant to the Citizen's Charter debate about the rights of citizens and the correlative duties of the state, to the extent that the powers of the royal prerogative are subject to no parliamentary control or scrutiny; nor can their use be easily challenged in the courts. Hence British subjects usually have no choice but to accept the use of the prerogative powers, unless a major abuse of them can be conclusively demonstrated. For example, ministers have on many occasions sought to resist the production in court of documents which parties to a case require in order to pursue their causes adequately, because their production is alleged to be contrary to the public interest. This assertion of the doctrine of Crown privilege (see Elcock, 1969) and the production of public immunity certificates to resist the production of internal memoranda in court, as occurred in the Matrix Churchill case, demands that the parties to the case accept the role of subjects: they cannot challenge the interest of the Crown as it is defined by Her Majesty's Ministers. In the Matrix Churchill case this could have entailed three business executives going to prison for something which demonstrably (as it turned out) did not constitute a criminal offence. However, the courts are now increasingly reluctant to accept claims of public interest immunity without challenge (Elcock, 1969; Griffith, 1977).

If one's view of human nature is less pessimistic than Hobbes's, it is highly undesirable that the state should have unlimited control over its subjects because there will then be no protection against unfair treatment, such as gender, racial or other discrimination and the suppression of otherwise legitimate opinions and demands. There are great dangers in allowing the state to assume R. N. Berki's (1979) transcendental role, in which it determines what individuals want and need. An example of this is the complete primacy accorded to the General Will in J. J. Rousseau's *Social Contract*. Here the individual is required to surrender his or her right of self-defence because if it is the General Will that I should die then I must accept this fate in the common interest under the terms of the Social Contract: shades of the death of Socrates. Instead, the state should be restricted to the instrumental role in which it is responsible for meeting citizens' expressed demands and needs. Hence subjects should be guaranteed a range of immunities with which the state has no right to interfere. The prerogative powers of the Crown potentially exceed this limit but since 1968 the courts have been increasingly vigilant in detecting and rejecting possible excesses or abuses of such powers. Nonetheless, the maintenance of public safety demands that citizens do to some degree behave as subjects, accepting without question the instructions given them by the police and other guardians of the legal and social order.

The *clients* of the public services are the more or less passive recipients of services provided for payment or free at the point of use, although in other contexts they may have more power: architects' clients, for example, dictate the kinds of buildings they require and the uses to which they are put. After this stage, however, the clients become dependent on the architect's ability and willingness to deliver what they require. In most public service contexts, however, clients have immunities against undue interference with their human rights and dignity but these may be transgressed where the role of service providers becomes unduly dominant, as Ivan Illich and others have argued in their analysis of 'disabling professionalism' (Illich, 1975; Illich et al., 1977). Service professionals may attach more importance to their accountability to their professional colleagues than to the wishes or interests of their clients. They observe above all an obligation to maintain 'good professional practice' and respect professional orthodoxies (see Gower Davies, 1972, for an interesting, if over-stated example). Clients may then be deprived of their autonomy and dignity by excessive, dominant intervention in their lives by professionals such as doctors, social workers or lawyers (Illich et al., 1977). Even in the case of the architect's client we discussed earlier, the client will at some stage have to accept without challenge the architect's advice that certain of his or her wishes, such as the use of a particular material or the adoption of a particular design feature, are impossible or impracticable.

Customers purchase goods and services through the market mechanism. James Connelly (1992) has argued that it is the exercise of market choice that distinguishes customers from consumers. They have certain rights, for instance that goods shall be safe and of merchantable quality and suppliers have the corresponding duty to meet these requirements. These rights may also be enforced through legislation and state supervision – hence the courts, tribunals or inspection agencies enforce the supplier's duty to the customer. Above all, customers have the right to choose whether or not to buy a particular product or to purchase it from a particular supplier.

Customers do not participate in decisions concerning the products they buy, except through the choices they make to buy or not to buy particular goods or service from a particular supplier. Thus customer influence occurs only through the market (price) mechanism and associated actions, such as responses to advertising. Hence, the relationship of customers with the state is individualized and the possibilities of collective enforcement of their rights or privileges disappear. Where a local authority has contracted out its services to the private sector and has thereby created a dismantled state, 'local authority service provision would be progressively replaced by a plurality of profit-seeking organizations providing for individualized customers' (Hambleton, 1992, p. 16). Customers can exercise some limited influence and seek redress by complaining when goods or services are unsatisfactory. The relationship between supplier and customer is regulated by an explicit or implied contract which defines the structure of rights and duties referred to above, which may be enforced through the judicial mechanisms of the state. However, many of the rights and privileges promised in the Citizen's Charter are not and perhaps cannot be enforced through the courts (Stowe, 1992). Furthermore, where public non-excludable or collective goods are concerned, there is no individual who can be identified as the customer.

Significantly, the current fashion in a range of public services, notably British Rail, is to refer to service recipients as customers. This is intended as a term indicating deference to the customer ('the customer is always right') but the customer has no right to participate in decisions about the service he or she is (or is not) provided with, except whether or not to purchase it. His or her choice of alternative suppliers is limited or non-existent. The scope of redress is therefore limited to the lodging of a complaint. Equally, the customer of the state often has no choice of supplier and this will often be the case with public services such as water, which are now provided by private companies. Also, they may have to accept the state's action whether they like it or not, for instance when arrested by the police or having a child taken into care by a court order. In the public services, the customer cannot by any means always be right. Here, the appropriate remedy for bad service or misuse of power is not a choice not to buy but to be able to seek redress through judicial processes or Ombudsmen or elected representatives who can be ejected from office by the citizens if they do not provide satisfaction.

Consumers are the recipients of goods and services, either through markets or by public (non-market) providers. Goods and services may be provided through prices determined by markets, subsidized prices or free allocation, the last two of which will entail some form of rationing unless the supply of the goods or service is abundant relative to the demand for it. Consumers may participate in collective decisions about service provision through market decisions or through consultation procedures, such as surveys and consultative committees. They also determine the extent to which public services are provided and funded by taxation, through the ballot box. Consumers have immunities which the suppliers of goods and services have no right to breach but they have no rights which impose corresponding duties on suppliers. As with customers, they may seek to enforce their immunities through the courts or other state regulators. Their participation in decisions concerning the supply of goods and services is confined at best to market research, which is discretionary on the part of the supplier and which is also selective, in that only those chosen to participate in the research, as respondents to a survey, are able to participate. Market research is in any case related only to the relationship between consumer and supplier. It confers no wider rights on the consumer, nor does it impose any duties on the supplier, who can take as much or as little notice of market research as he or she thinks fit.

Connelly (1992) has argued that consumerism in the public services can be no more than a 'general ethical goal' rather than being a commitment to ensure that 'an enterprise provides the goods and services that customers want at the quantity, quality and manner in which they want them' (1992, p. 30). This is because in the public services, consumers often cannot exercise market choice because they cannot choose alternative suppliers or alternative mixes of price and quality. Also, supply may have to be rationed through a system other than the price mechanism, for instance a waiting list. Hence, instead their rights as citizens must be recognized (Connelly, 1992, pp. 30–31).

The key word which is used again and again in the above discussion is 'accountability'. It is a complex concept which defines the network of relationships between individuals or organizations which determines their rights and duties relative to one another. It includes at least three dimensions that need to be considered by those who are responsible for providing public sector goods and services (Elcock and Haywood, 1980: Elcock, 1991):

- Accountability *upwards* to superior officers and ultimately to elected representatives where the goods or service is provided by a government agency. However, in private firms accountability is upwards to managers and shareholders, who have no obvious common interest with the firm's customers and seek a different goal: profit maximization. By contrast, the public sector's customers are also voters and citizens with a right to demand that someone be held to account when mistakes are made and to change the top management at the next general or local election (Gyford, 1991).
- Accountability *outwards* to professional or other colleagues, which may be exercised within the public services (for example, almost all town and country planners), in the private sector (shopkeepers, many lawyers and accountants) or across both the public and private domains, for instance architects (Dunleavy, 1980). If accountability outwards becomes too strong relative to the other directions of accountability, 'disabling

professionalism' may result, when clients are treated in accordance with established professional norms or practice, whether or not that treatment is likely to be beneficial or harmful to the client (Illich et al., 1977). For example, Illich (1975) states that some 15 per cent of hospital admissions are the result of iatrogenesis: mistakes made by doctors.

- Accountability *downwards* to those receiving goods and services, whether as citizens, clients, customers or consumers. The nature and regulation of this relationship is different in the differing contexts of citizenship, subjection, servicing clients, serving customers or satisfying consumers. The behaviour of the supplier, especially of the 'front-line' staff who deal directly with the recipients of goods or services, must and will vary depending on whether the recipients are regarded as citizens, subjects, clients, customers or consumers. Staff will treat citizens, who have the right to complain to elected representatives and through other channels, differently from subjects who have no such rights. Indeed, the combination of arrogance and insensitivity which some public servants display in their dealings with the public, which Hoggett and Hambleton (1987) describe as 'bureaucratic paternalism', is arguably one of the main reasons why public confidence in the public services declined in the 1970s (Elcock, 1991). The Major government's response has been to expose public services to market forces through privatization, de-regulation or competitive tendering thus, it is argued, changing clients into customers by extending market choice into many public services where it did not operate previously. Economic choice through the market therefore replaces political choice through the medium of elections. Alternatively, public authorities have sought to develop sensitivity to consumers through market research, decentralization, consumer awareness programmes and similar means to bring themselves closer to their clients, which J. D. Stewart (1986) has called the public service orientation (see also Gyford, 1991).

Acountability downwards is arguably the main concern of the Citizen's Charter and the many related service charters because they are concerned to strengthen service recipients' ability to complain and obtain redress where public services are unsatisfactory or worse. They have less to say about accountability outwards and nothing to say about accountability upwards to citizens through their elected representatives. Hence, the extent to which the Citizen's Charter extends or strengthens the rights of members of the public, relates only to the rights of consumers or customers rather than those of citizens.

We can now relate the rights and duties of citizens or consumers to the various directions of accountability relationships. This task is important because the state is responsible for providing public, non-excludable goods and services, as well as because it provides a varying number and range of private or excludable goods and services as determined by the elected government of the day in accordance with its ideological preferences and the pressures imposed upon it by citizens and interest groups.

Citizens both possess rights within and are controlled by frameworks of accountability upwards, downwards and outwards. Their right and duty to participate, and the privileges associated with them, give citizens the ability to seek redress and influence public policies through democratic and representative processes which constitute the ultimate form of accountability upwards for all public servants. Citizens also determine the balance of provision between the public and private sectors, by choosing political parties who favour more or less provision of private or excludable goods by the public sector. They can also hold them accountable downwards through legal, quasi-legal and administrative redress procedures including the courts, administrative tribunals and ombudsmen.

In such a system, the accountability outwards of professionals and others in the public services should be held in check by accountability upwards and downwards because the rights of the citizen impose corresponding and wide ranging duties on the state and its servants. The behaviour of public servants has traditionally been held in check by a particular form of accountability outwards: a series of expectations, especially among civil servants, as to the proper conduct of public servants which have long ensured that they conduct themselves honestly and without favouritism (Chapman, 1988a; Hennessy, 1989). However, these norms have been weakened by the changes in managing the public services that have occurred in recent years. These may have increased the initiative available to and exercised by public service managers but at the risk of weakening the defences of public servants against impropriety and corruption (Chapman, 1988b). Significantly, in the light of lapses in conduct by ministers and others, a code of ethics for civil servants has now had to be drawn up (*The Guardian*, 27 January 1995).

Subjects cannot hold the state accountable; attempts to do so will be construed as *lèse-majesté*, and as such, will be punished. Hence the use made of the prerogative powers of the Crown are difficult or impossible to challenge, either in the courts or in parliament. At most, subjects enjoy limited immunities but there is no guarantee that the state will observe its corresponding liabilities to respect its subjects' immunities. This was very evident when the home secretary's power to authorize the interception of mail or the tapping of telephones was part of the royal prerogative and was therefore not subject to accountability to parliament or anyone else. This power is now regulated by legislation as a consequence of a government defeat before the European Court of Human Rights but this has not materially reduced the extent of the Home Secretary's discretion; nor has it materially increased the effectiveness of redress where the powers may have been misused (Hewitt, 1982). Effective accountability in any direction does not exist.

Clients are given some rights and immunities through which they can hold service providers accountable both upwards through their representatives and downwards through redress procedures. However, they will tend to be the passive recipients of services provided by officials whose first concern may or may not be the client's benefit. They are not likely to be encouraged to complain or seek redress. If the Citizen's Charter and its associated service specific charters encourage clients to behave more like citizens by enabling and encouraging them to assert their rights and lodging complaints, so much the better.

Customers can enforce accountability downwards where they are given legally enforceable rights to expect satisfactory goods or services, for example through statutes that impose duties on suppliers to provide goods and services that are of adequate standard, safe and of merchantable quality but there is no structure of accountability upwards or outwards, except through market mechanisms. Consumers can only enforce accountability downwards but increasingly public authorities are accepting that they should take heed of their consumers' feelings, needs and wishes. However, in these cases participation is an opportunity but not a right.

The dominance of market solutions seems likely to become at least somewhat diluted through the development of the increased concern to improve the accessibility and acceptability of the public services, which is reflected in the development of the Citizen's Charter. The Prime Minister has himself declared that

> . . . to make public services answer better to the wishes of their users and to raise their quality overall, have been ambitions of mine ever since I was a local councillor in Lambeth over 20 years ago (Cabinet Office, 1991, p. 2).

This is the fundamental purpose of the Citizen's Charter but careful thought needs to be given to whether we are seeking to strengthen the essentially participative role of the citizen, or simply to increase the protective rights, privileges and immunities accorded to customers. On this decision will depend whether effort is put mainly into improving customer services at the 'street level' of public service agencies (Lipsky, 1980), or whether citizens are to be encouraged to become more active participants in influencing the policies and management of the public services they pay for and use – whether voluntarily or otherwise. The implications of doing the latter are much more fundamental for the management of public services than are those of the former. However, they are not addressed in the Citizen's Charter, which in short, is concerned with the improvement of accountability downwards but has little to say about accountability upwards and outwards.

References

Aristotle (1962), *The Politics*, ed. T. A. Sinclair, Penguin, London.

Berki, R. N. (1979), 'State and Society: an Antithesis of Modern Political Thought', in Berki, R. N. and Hayward, J. E. S. (eds), *State and Society in Contemporary Europe*, Martin Robertson, Oxford.

Chapman, R. A. (1988a), *Ethics in the Civil Service*, Routledge, London.

Chapman, R. A. (1988b), *The Art of Darkness*, inaugural lecture, University of Durham.

Cabinet Office (1991), *The Citizen's Charter: Raising the Standard*, Cm 1599, HMSO, London.

Connelly, J. (1992), 'All Customers Now? Consumerism in the Public Service', *Teaching Public Administration*, vol. 12, no. 2, pp. 29–32.

Dunleavy, P. (1980), *Urban Political Analysis*, Macmillan, London.

Elcock, H. J. (1969), 'Justice and the Political Order', *Political Studies*, vol. 17, pp. 394–412.

Elcock, H. J. (1986), *Local Government: Politicians, Professionals and the Public in Local Authorities*, 2nd edn, Routledge, London.

Elcock, H. J. (1991), *Change and Decay? Public Administration in the 1990s*, Routledge, London.

Elcock, H. J. (1995), 'The Fallacies of Management', in *Public Policy and Administration*, vol. 10, no. 1, Spring 1995, pp. 34–48.

Elcock, H. and Haywood, S. (1980), *The Buck Stops Where? Accountability and Control in the National Health Service*, University of Hull, Hull.

Fenwick, J. and Harrop, H. (1988), *Consumer Responses to Local Authority Services: Notes Towards an Operational Model*, Local Authority Management Unit Discussion Paper No. 88/1, Newcastle-upon-Tyne Polytechnic, Newcastle-upon-Tyne.

Gower Davies, J. (1972), *The Evangelistic Bureaucrat*, Tavistock Press, London.

Griffith, J. A. G. (1977), *The Politics of the Judiciary*, Fontana/Collins, London.

Gyford, J. (1991), *Citizens, Consumers and Councils: Local Government and the Public*, Macmillan, London.

Hambleton, R. (1992), 'Decentralization and Democracy in Local Government', *Public Money and Management*, vol. 12, no. 3, pp. 9–20.

Heater, Derek (1992), 'Civis Britannicus Sum', *Parliamentary Affairs*, vol. 45, no. 3, pp. 439–440.

Held, David (1992), 'Democracy: From City States to Cosmopolitan Order?', *Political Studies*, vol. 60, Special Issue: Prospects for Democracy, pp. 10–39.

Hennessy, P. (1989), *Whitehall*, 2nd edn, Fontana Books, London.

Hewitt, P. (1982), *The Abuse of Power*, Martin Robertson, London.

Hobbes, Thomas (1968), *Leviathan*, Penguin, Harmondsworth.

Hoggett, P. and Hambleton, R., (eds), (1987), *Decentralisation and Democracy*, School of Advanced Urban Studies, Bristol.

Hohfeld, W. N. (1919), *Fundamental Legal Conceptions as Applied in Judicial Reasoning*, Yale University Press, New Haven.

Illich, Ivan (1975), *Medical Nemesis: The Medical Expropriation of Health*, Calder and Boyars, London.

Illich, Ivan et al. (1977), *Disabling Professions*, Boyars, London.

Jones, G. and Stewart, J. D. (1984), *The Struggle for Local Government*, Allen and Unwin, London.

Lipskey, M. (1980), *Street Level Bureaucracy*, Russell Sage, London.

Lovell, R. (1992), 'Citizen's Charter: The Cultural Challenge', *Public Administration*, vol. 70, pp. 395–404.

McCloskey, R. G. (1960), *The United States Supreme Court*, University of Chicago Press, Chicago.

Mill, J. S. (1972), *Representative Government*, Dent, London.

Rousseau, J. J. (1968), *The Social Contract,* ed. M. Cranston, Penguin, Harmondsworth.

Savage, S. (1990), 'Law and Order Policy', in Savage, S. and Robins, L. (eds), *Public Policy under Thatcher*, Macmillan, London.

Stacey, F. (1975), *A New Bill of Rights for Britain*, David and Charles, Newton Abbott.

Stewart, J. D. (1986), *The New Management of Local Government*, Allen and Unwin, London.

Stowe, K. (1992), 'Good Piano Won't Play Bad Music: Administrative Reform and Good Governance', *Public Administration*, vol. 70, pp. 387–394.

Street, H. (1963), *Freedom, the Individual and the Law*, Penguin Books, Harmondsworth.

Taylor, L. C. J. (1992), Richard Dimbleby Lecture, BBC 1 Television, 30 November 1992.

Thornley, A. (1990), *Urban Planning under Thatcher*, Routledge, London.

4 Citizens and Customer Care

J. A. CHANDLER

As both John Kingdom and Howard Elcock observe in this volume, the Citizen's Charter encapsulates a rather curious notion of the concept of a 'citizen'. This may reflect the fact that whilst documents outlining the idea do not use the term 'customer', the Charter is framed more as a means of ensuring the better delivery of services to those who consume and, in general, pay for that service, rather than advancing any means to improve the lot of the individual as citizen. The initiative might, therefore, be better termed a 'customers' charter.

This chapter considers the implication of the enthusiasm of the late 1980s and early 1990s concerning the invention or discovery of the public service customer. It is suggested that this is not the most felicitous development in public administration. It will be argued that, first, 'customer' as used in the private sector is more a legitimating concept than a statement of any deference to the needs and wishes of service purchasers; secondly, it is difficult if not impossible in the public sector to define who is a 'customer'; thirdly, it is usually impossible and often undesirable for the public sector to ever satisfy its service recipients, and, finally, the use of the concept is profoundly undemocratic.

We are all consumers now

Just as we discover at some point that without knowing it we have been talking prose throughout our lives, in the late 1980s many of us discovered we had, unbeknown to us, been customers of many public services. Concern for customer care emerged as an important issue in the public sector only in the 1980s and was connected closely with the new business and public choice orientation towards government brought into play by the Thatcher and Reagan administrations. The development of this approach has, however, been rapid in terms of the language and rhetoric of public service provision.

Travelling by British Rail we ceased to be passengers and were greeted as customers, in many of the more business-orientated universities enthusiastic new management administrators began talking of customers as opposed to students. Even traffic wardens are encouraged to refer to the owners of illegally parked cars as customers.[1]

The concept of 'the customer' has been developed not only in government and agency speak but has also become accepted terminology to refer to some recipients of public services in academic discourse. John Stewart (1988) and Clarke and Stewart, academic pioneers in the adoption of this term within public sector analysis, stress the need for 'an active relationship between the [local] authority and the public, both as customer and citizen' (1990, p. 25). Their emphasis on individuals as citizens is an important antidote to tendencies that suggest that individuals are solely self-interested consumers. Public sector theorists tend, however, to refer to 'consumerism' as denoting economic, self-interested behaviour and 'citizenship' as politically orientated collective action (Gyford, 1991). In the United States, however, the more aggressively managerialist *Reinventing Government* by Osborne and Gaebler (1992) has no such reticence concerning the primacy of the public service 'customer'.

The Citizen's Charter

Whilst the Citizen's Charter does not explicitly use the language of the customer as king, this sentiment is embedded in the rhetoric of its founding documents. The introduction to the first report on the Citizen's Charter document under the signature of the Prime Minister clearly indicates this consumer-orientated approach.

> The Citizen's Charter sees public services through the eyes of those who use them. For too long the provider has dominated and now it is the turn of the user . . . The principles of the Citizen's Charter, simple but tough, are increasingly accepted. They give the citizen published standards and results; choice and competition as a spur to quality improvement; responsiveness; and value for money to get the best possible service with the resources the nation can afford. They give more power to the citizen and more freedom to choose (Cabinet Office, 1992).

The report later indicates that the initiative will 'raise quality, increase choice, secure better value and extend accountability' (Cabinet Office, 1992, p. 1).

The government papers that outline the idea of the Citizen's Charter (Cabinet Office, 1991, 1992) pay, therefore, little attention to the wider aspects of citizenship but suggest that public services ought to be primarily orientated to serving the needs of their consumers.

The customer in the private sector

There are many popular studies of management that appear to place the customer in a central role in determining the aims and objectives of an enterprise. Drucker, for example, argues that 'it is the customer who determines what a business is' (1977, p. 90). Peters and Waterman observe that:

> The good news from the excellent companies is the extent to which, and the intensity with which, the customers intrude into every nook and cranny of the business-sales, manufacturing, research, accounting (1982, p. 156).

Despite the celebration of the centrality of the customer from the likes of Drucker (1977, 1986, 1989), and Peters and Waterman (1982) and Peters and Austin (1986), many textbooks on management that are concerned less with providing sensational new aphorisms for ambitious managers, than with describing the mundane realities of the business world, give little space for discussion of the role of customers in shaping a business. A trawl of management literature would suggest that probably the great majority of writers in this genre do not see customer needs as the central purpose of a business organization. For example, Porter's studies of competitive advantage do not place customer care as a central issue as opposed to policy on pricing or the capacity of a business to differentiate its output from that of possible competitors (Porter, 1985, 1990). Standard texts on strategic management, Johnson and Scholes (1989) for example, similarly make little comment on the role of the customer.

On occasion, some writers show a clear awareness of their doubts about the centrality of customers in determining business strategy and suggest that the customer cannot be the determinant of business development. As Arthur Sharplin observes:

> It is common to seem to place the customer first by saying something like, only through serving customers can a company exist and prosper in the long run. If, exist and prosper means provide a high return to shareholders in

future years, then serving the shareholder is the primary goal and the customer is merely a means to that end (Sharplin, 1985, p. 51).

As Sharplin is aware, if the customers' needs are fully satisfied by providing as good a quality product as possible at the lowest price, then the supplier will be forced to cut heavily into profit margins to the extent that the business will not make money for its shareholders. Indeed, many businesses have flourished not because they have placed the customer's needs at the centre of their concern but because they have either manipulated the market to give themselves a monopoly position, or provided an image for their product unrelated to its real cost and quality. Care for the customer extends only so far as to ensure that the business retains a capacity to secure from them its own utility.

The majority of strategic management theorists, therefore, place the customer as but one (often minor) variable among the many factors that determine the growth and profitability of a business. Of equal, if not greater importance than the customer is the need to eliminate competition, respond to environmental changes or accommodate new legislation and technological change, and improve internal efficiency in manufacturing and marketing techniques. In addition to these factors, which are essential concerns for the promotion of a successful business strategy, many bureaucrats in both private and public organizations have, as public choice theorists observe, personal agendas to promote their own security or maximize the ratio of income to effort that may be counter-productive to the fortunes of the business (Niskanen, 1971).

A business that orientated its activities solely towards the aim of satisfying its customers would, therefore, quickly cease to serve the interests of its shareholders, fail to make profits and join the ranks of failed companies. Such a firm would probably have also fallen foul of the numerous government regulations that are designed to prevent injustices that may arise through satisfying customers' needs to the detriment of employees and the public at large.

The values of customer care

Although the values of 'customer care' must be but one of several strategic issues that need to be borne in mind by a profit-making business, the idea does have considerable importance. Clearly, all other factors being equal, it makes sense to satisfy the demands of customers within a private sector business as far as possible within the constraints laid down by other demands upon the organization. Dissatisfied customers will seek alternative suppliers and their departure will undermine the economic viability of the enterprise. Customers who believe, rightly or wrongly, that they are the centre of a company's concern will generally be warmly drawn into further support for the business by purchasing its products and encouraging others to do so. Good customer relationships, therefore, have considerable importance in creating a climate of support and legitimacy for the business.

In addition to this clear and sensible objective, pursuit of customer care may have further but less obvious functions. Monitoring customer reactions and complaints can have an important role in facilitating senior management's capacity to monitor and control their enterprise. Senior managers can, for example, set objectives for their enterprise on, for example, the quality of the product and monitor the extent to which their aims are met by assessing the volume of complaints from the public. They can then use this data as a means of pressurizing more junior managers to implement their objectives.

A further and less immediately crucial function of customer care is to create a climate that helps legitimize market capitalism in general. Close attention to the needs of customers is a virtue that is most advantageously not hidden under bushels but marketed widely so as to create a favourable public image for a company. Customer care, promoting a belief that an enterprise is working for the greater good of individuals and society in general, creates a valuable legitimizing myth for the capitalist system that may help defend private enterprise against the demands that can be made by central government. The succession of television commercials, sponsorships, bill boards and newspaper adverts suggesting that each individual life insurance company, hair care product or better mousetrap will enhance our standard of life are inescapable for much of our waking lives. This incessant feed of consumerist propaganda probably has a more significant role in establishing the legitimacy of private enterprise than any policies and statements of capitalist governments.

The public sector customer

The preceding critique of the role of the 'customer' as a determinant of private sector business strategy may, paradoxically, be used as an argument to suggest that the primacy of customer care is of more, rather than less, importance within the public than the private sector. Given that private businesses are primarily concerned with profitability, customer care becomes a means to an end and cannot be the guiding principle around which to organize the strategy of the business. In contrast, within the many public sector organizations that are not legally required to make a profit, it may be suggested that customer care can be a far more important and central objective.

If this argument is accepted then much of the rationale of government policy towards the public sector becomes a hindrance rather than an asset in securing greater sensitivity of public services to the needs and requirements of the citizen. As the government presses for extensive privatization of services and, failing this, to ensure that other services in the public domain are paid for by direct charges imposed on users, the delivery of public services is increasingly forced to mirror private sector practice with its ulterior motives towards customer care.

The Citizen's Charter is itself suffused with an enthusiasm for privatization. Behind the gloss of concern for the consumer lies the government's conviction that the principal route to ensuring better services is through competition between privately owned suppliers. The Charter documents observe that:

> . . . where choice and competition are limited, consumers cannot as easily and effectively make their views count. In many public services, therefore, we need to increase both choice and competition where we can . . . Many of Britain's key industries and public services have been privatized in the last decade. This has been done in a way which promotes direct competition between providers as far as possible. Where elements of monopoly remain regulation protects the consumer (Cabinet Office, 1991, p. 3).

In promoting the Citizen's Charter, the government appears, therefore, to have little confidence in the argument that a public non-profit-making service will have a greater capacity to deliver services in line with popular opinion than a private sector concern.

Who is the public service customer?

Although the idea of customer care as applied to non-profit-making public services may be more plausible than the legitimizing device as applied to private sector services, there are, nevertheless, a number of serious problems with translating a concept that has some meaning within private sector competitive businesses to public provision.

Within the private sector it is usually a simple matter to define the customers of any enterprise. These are the individuals who purchase a particular product or service from a business. Within the public sector it is much more difficult to establish the customer by reference to a basic contractual market-based relationship.

In a few cases within the public sector it can, at least superficially, be relatively easy to identify a supplier/customer exchange relationship, even though this may stretch our previously accepted habits of language. Thus, a train passenger pays for a specific service from British Rail and can be regarded as a customer in the same way as an individual is a customer when purchasing vegetables from the grocer or insurance from a bank. However, even in this sector it may be argued that the nationalization of rail services was not undertaken as a consequence of irrational socializing dogma but, in part at least, as a reflection of the importance rail services have for the economy and social mobility as a whole. Poor rail services affect not only the individual traveller but indirectly the many individuals and groups dependent on an efficient and relatively inexpensive national transport system.

In other spheres of public sector provision the immediate and direct recipient of public services can only be conceived as the customer by extending considerably the boundaries of credulity. This problem applies extensively in the sphere of the adjudication and enforcement of law. It makes no sense to suggest that the traffic warden is providing for the individual needs of an irate motorist. Unlike travellers on British Rail there is no mutually beneficial contractual relationship between the traffic warden and the illegally parked motorist. Similarly, prisoners or suspects in a criminal enquiry are hardly receiving a service to fulfil their needs as individuals.

The role of the law enforcement and judicial agencies may be argued to be for the benefit of the public at large rather than the individuals who are directly ministered to by such agencies. This concept of a collective 'customer' however, makes little sense in relation to the normal private sector usage of the term where the customer/supplier relationship is one of contractual payment and receipt for goods and services. Individuals other than the customer and supplier may benefit from a commercial transaction but these third-party beneficiaries will not be regarded by the supplier as their 'customers'. An individual may benefit from the construction of a new fence by a neighbour but he or she will not be regarded as the customer by the supplier of fences. If, therefore, the term 'customer' is used to describe third-party beneficiaries of a public service, it is to use the term in a very different sense from its usage in private sector discourse.

It may, however, be argued that the term 'customer' makes sense in the public sector if it is regarded as denoting an individual who has paid for a service either individually or through a collective contribution. However, since many recipients of public services do not contribute to the taxes that pay for those services it is, similarly, difficult to sustain this view, let alone translate it into a means of enhancing 'customer care'.

How is it possible to satisfy the public customer?

Defining customers in terms of shared public services is, therefore, to ask an improper question and receive an improper answer. The improper answer then propels the argument of customer care down an even more illogical path. The private sector argument valuing the role of the customer may be expressed simplistically in the view that the customer is always right. In the somewhat more sophisticated aphorisms of Peters and Waterman (1982), a successful business achieves its goals in part by being close to its customers, understanding their desires and fulfilling their needs through the supply of appropriate quality goods and services.

It is, however, by no means possible for a non-profit-making public organization to simplistically serve the general public as if they were customers whose needs must be fully satisfied any more than this naive idea makes sense within the private sector. Any government agency will be restricted in its capacity to deliver, for example, refuse collection or health care by numerous technical factors and by the resources it has available to meet needs and overcome such constraints. In this context, a service operated by a public or private organization will be in a similar position of having to cut the quality of service according to the cloth provided.

A quality domestic refuse collection organization will, for example, provide an ideal service if it collects refuse from a house as frequently as is demanded by its occupants, provides the type of refuse container preferred by the householder and not, as is normal, a standard issue dustbin or plastic sack, and collects the container from wherever the householder wishes to place the receptacle, even if this necessitates refuse collectors lugging heavy bins round tortuous gardens and drives. In practice no refuse-collecting concern, whether operated privately or publicly, will normally provide such a service since the cost would be prohibitive.

The provision of refuse services geared to customer needs is made even more difficult because it is essential for the wider good of securing the public from infectious disease, environmental pollution and the expansion of the rodent population to ensure that every householder participates in some refuse collecting service, whether they like it or not. Customers cannot have the right to choose to pay less for sub-standard services if, by taking this option, they endanger the health of their neighbours. Allowing refuse collection or environmental health services to be items bought by consumers in accord with their capacity to pay and their individual preferences for value for money would quickly lead to the degeneration of many essential public services to hazardous levels.

The notion of customer care driving a public sector supplier into ensuring that services provide the best possible arrangement for the consumer is wholly inapplicable to the supply of collectively consumed public goods and services. There is no clear sense in which the individuals directly receiving a service can be regarded as customers any more than the public as a collectivity can be treated as customers. As a consequence it becomes impossible to determine using the rhetoric of securing customer satisfaction how a service should be delivered to satisfy what is but a chimera.

Alternative functions of the Citizen's Charter

Given that the concept of the 'customer' is hard to define in relation to collective public services and that the notion of responding to the customers' needs is, consequently, even harder to operationalize, it may be questioned whether Major's big idea is simply a product of well meaning but confused thinking. Is the government simply seeking to improve the quality of public services using the rather ill-advised but immediately populist language of private sector management?

In practical terms the principal innovation of the strategy has been to establish structures for measuring certain aspects of performance output by public organizations, making these measures public and creating schemes for compensating members of the public who feel they have not received a service of the standard expected from these targets. Compensation for failure to achieve management-determined standards of service can be viewed as a very modest extension of public accountability or as a means to improve standards of provision.

However, some reservations may be made about the method of securing this modest goal. The quality targets devised for particular services appear to be skilfully crafted not by the general public but by senior managers of the services that have chosen to take up the charter initiative. Under such circumstances managers will set themselves targets they wish to see achieved once they have strategically balanced the conflicting demands of quality provision, resources and external legal and technical restraints that affect their business. Thus, as Peter Curwen demonstrates in this volume, British Rail set different standards of attainment for different rail routes, even though a traveller on Southern Railways will require as perfect a standard of time keeping as on any other rail route.

The Citizen's Charter may, therefore, perhaps be seen simply as a useful device for ensuring that senior public managers establish systems to monitor the performance of their more junior managers responsible for the immediate delivery of a service to the public and have cause to improve their efficiency should they fail to meet targets.

Customer care as a legitimizing myth

The use of charters as a system of management control may generally be viewed as a welcome means of securing more reliable and efficient delivery of services. There are, however, further and far more seriously political aspects of the initiative that should be viewed with some concern.

The idea of regarding citizens as consumers has a legitimating value that is unlikely to be lost on populist governments. The legitimizing values of 'customer care' as used in the private sector can readily be translated through the charters into a means of legitimizing new private sector styles of management in the public sector. Thus, for example, the problem of loss of public accountability that may result from the privatization of rail services can be offset if the public are led to believe that accountability is retained through the legitimating device of a charter that guarantees them the benefits of 'customer care'. If social service clients are persuaded to believe they are valued customers they may think the treatment and the help that they are grudgingly provided with are the best possible services that they can be given.

At a more general and seriously damaging level this development of a legitimizing myth of customer care can be a powerful device for undermining collective rather than individualist thought. Citizens may be manoeuvred into a belief that they can demand a centrally specified level of treatment as a customer of the government and be oblivious to their right to help collectively determine what that standard should be. Government can best dominate society if each citizen accepts that they are atomized individuals dealing with a service provider on an individual basis.

An erosion of democratic values

The most serious concern over the establishment of the Citizen's Charter should be that it implies a serious critique of the role and function of liberal democracy in Britain. The minister responsible for establishing the initiative, William Waldegrave, appears to have recognized this role very explicitly, observing in 1993:

> Services are not necessarily made responsive to the public simply by giving citizens a democratic voice and a distant one at that, in their make up. They can be made responsive by giving the public choices, or by instituting mechanisms which build in publicly approved standards and redress when they are not attained (quoted in Walsh, 1995, p. xvi).

There appears, at least among some influential founders of the Citizen's Charter, a lack of confidence that liberal democracy as presently constituted in Britain can secure responsivity of the elected to the citizen. As Walsh observes, 'the exercise of choice in the marketplace for public service is seen as more effective than the use of the vote' (1995, p. xv).

It should be evident from the preceding discussions that there are serious problems with ensuring sensitivity of public services by reference to customers in the market place. It is, as argued above, difficult, if not illogical, to identify who actually is the 'customer' for many publicly provided services. Operating in such an ambiguous morass, emphasis on customer care allows the government to be arbiter of who is the customer and, therefore, whose interests should be catered for and who should be excluded from consideration concerning the standards of service provision.

Most corrosively, such an arrangement sees government as a device for providing specific services to individuals on a contractual basis and establishing a system that allows those receiving the service set by the government to complain if they do not get what the government has promised. This gives the citizen but a fraction of what is necessary within a democracy.

It excludes the public from any voice in the more fundamental decisions about what services ought to be delivered, at what standard and at what cost.

In the imaginary world of perfect market competition consumers may complain about an inadequate product and affect the inadequate business by purchasing from an alternative supplier who is more capable of responding to consumer needs. Such a pattern is wholly inapplicable for public sector provision, which in general supplies services that cannot be subject to the laws of perfect competition.

Governments come into being because those in power consider that communities need collective services such as defence or education, which cannot or should not be obtained through market-place transactions. Democratic government ensures that the nature of these services are determined with reference to public opinion rather than the arbitrary views of a self-perpetuating elite or to the inequalities of the market place. A democracy must ensure that the range of services offered by the public sector, as opposed to the private sector, is determined by a government responsive to public opinion. Such a government must also determine who should receive a particular service, the standard at which the service is provided and who should be asked to pay for its provision.

Thus, the standard of health care provision in Britain, for example, cannot be left to a private sector market that would allow the wealthy to buy a high standard of care and the poorest to receive no provision at all. Given the need for publicly provided health care, a democracy cannot allow the public the right to object only when standards set by the government are not obtained. A democratic health care system requires that the quantity and type of health care provided by government, the priorities given to each group requiring publicly provided health care and the costs of meeting the required standards are set through a process of public debate and public decision making.

Since the government is tending towards a view that many more publicly provided services should be paid for through charges imposed on the public who directly consume that service, there are dangers of an even more inegalitarian and undemocratic twist to the values within the Citizen's Charter. Taken to its fullest development, only those with the capacity to pay will be in receipt of public services and the capacity to affect the standard of service through customer complaints will also, therefore, be reserved to those who can pay. Democratic government based on individualist contractual arrangements for safeguarding rights is a highly inegalitarian form of government. As many theorists such as Dahl (1989) in his later writings or Held (1987) point out, an effective democracy that leads to fewer inequalities and greater opportunities for the individual in society cannot be based on a simple market-based contractual formula.

Public services should be established so as to benefit majority opinions in society and be operated so that policies concerning their delivery and the costs of supply reflect, and are accountable to, public opinion in general and not simply the recipient of a service. The concept of democracy, unlike that of customer sovereignty, does not single out a particular group as the beneficiaries of a service but is a concept that is applied to collective action. The idea of democratic accountability can make sense in analysing problems of the appropriate balance of gain between those who are in receipt of public goods or public action and those who gain collectively by that provision and those who must resource the service. If the values of pluralist democracy work in practice there is little need, therefore, to introduce into the rhetoric of public sector analysis the meaningless and inoperable private-sector-based concept of the 'customer'.

It can, of course, be argued that liberal democracy in Britain is far from what it should be and is in much need of repair. There is, however, no chance of securing better responsivity and accountability of policy-makers to the public by the introduction of consumer care and the inapplicable values of the Citizen's Charter.

If the government were seriously concerned with improving democracy in Britain there are many alternative strategies they could consider that might ensure greater accountability and sensitivity of public service provision to the citizen. These could include, as Michael Hunt observes in a later chapter, more open government; they may also involve, as Dave Morris describes, serious attention to issue of quality management; also important may be better civic education to ensure the public have a heightened awareness of their rights and duties within the state. Decentralization of decision-making over local services to communities would also greatly facilitate greater sensitivity of public provision to those who collectively or individually depend on these services. There are also numerous structural measures that may allow greater accountability of quangos through the democratization of the many state-established autocracies that litter the British administrative system or the redemocratization of major now privatized utilities such as gas, water and electricity supply.

Conclusion

The rhetoric of customer care and consumerism even when applied to the private sector is, if taken in isolation from the concern for profitability, technical limitations and resource capacity of a business, simply managerial nonsense. Within the public sector, where it is often impossible to distinguish the consumer from the citizen and general public, such talk is even greater nonsense.

The Citizen's Charter and similar efforts by government to ensure that bureaucracies are more sensitive to consumer demand are far from what they seem. They tend to be devices that move large bureaucracies from the public to the private sector, legitimizing them with a veneer of a complaints procedure that serves more as an internal organizational control device for senior managers than a system to benefit consumers.

One of the most unfortunate results of such practice has been for the government to divert public interest away from schemes developed in the public sector that may genuinely enhance the development of democracy in Britain. It may also be questioned whether such a device is part of an agenda to replace electoral democracy with consumerism as the basis of the relationship between those in power and the citizen who pays for a public service.

Note

1. Interview with consultant broadcast on BBC Radio 4's 'PM' programme, 21 January 1993.

References

Clarke, M. and Stewart, J. (1990), *General Management in Local Government: Getting the Balance Right*, Longman, Harlow.

Dahl, R.A. (1989), *Democracy and its Critics*, Yale University Press, New Haven, CT.

Drucker, P. (1977), *People and Performance*, Heinemann, London.

Drucker, P. (1986), *The Frontiers of Management*, Heinemann, London.

Drucker, P. (1989), *The New Realities*, Heinemann, London.

Gyford, J. (1991), *Citizens, Consumers and Councils*, Macmillan, London.

Held, D. (1987), *Models of Democracy*, Polity Press, Cambridge.

Cabinet Office (1991), *The Citizen's Charter: Raising the Standard*, Cm 1599, HMSO, London.

Cabinet Office (1992), *The Citizen's Charter: First Report*, Cm 2101, HMSO, London.

Johnson, G. and Scholes, K. (1989), *Exploring Corporate Strategy*, 3rd edn, Prentice Hall, London.

Niskanen, W.A. (1971), *Bureaucracy and Representative Government*, Aldine-Atherton, Chicago.

Osborne, D. and Gaebler, T. (1992), *Reinventing Government*, Addison-Wesley, Reading, MA.

Peters, T. and Austin, N. (1986), *A Passion for Excellence*, Fontana, London.

Peters, T. and Waterman, R.H. (1982), *In Search of Excellence*, Harper and Row, London.

Porter, M. (1985), *Competitive Advantage*, Free Press, New York.

Porter, M. (1990), *The Competitive Advantage of Nations*, Macmillan, London.

Sharplin, A. (1985), *Strategic Management*, McGraw Hill, New York.

Stewart, J. (1988), *Understanding the Management of Local Government*, Longman, Harlow.

Walsh, K. (1995), *Public Services and Market Mechanisms*, Macmillan, London.

5 Accountability, Openness and the Citizen's Charter

MICHAEL HUNT

The Foreword to the Citizen's Charter makes its intentions quite clear. It is about giving the people 'more say in how their services are run'. It is about 'giving more power to the citizen'; it is 'a testament of our belief in people's right to be informed and choose for themselves'. Phrases such as these imply some commitment to a more open system of government which would enable citizens both to have more information about services provided for them and also to have a greater say in how they are run. This chapter examines the government's real commitment to this through the content of the Charter and also, more broadly, through its attitude to openness as expressed in the White Paper on open government (Cabinet Office, 1993).

The Citizen's Charter was published as a White Paper in June 1991. According to the introduction its purpose is to 'set out the mechanics for improving choice, quality, value and accountability' (Cabinet Office, 1991, p. 4). The assumption must be that these words are linked in some way although their precise meanings are left to the reader to derive since they are not explained in the text. 'Choice', for example, is linked to the desirable objective that the public should be consulted about the way in which their services are provided, thus presumably increasing accountability. The document notes a need 'to increase both choice and competition', and sees this as a way to ensure quality in the provision of services. Other parts of the introduction give further clues as to how quality will be encouraged and maintained. There is mention of the publication of information on standards achieved, tougher independent inspectorates, more effective complaints procedures, and more redress for the citizen when things go wrong. 'Value' is hardly referred to except in terms of 'quality'. The introduction refers to the citizen as a taxpayer (Cabinet Office, 1991, p. 4) and argues that taxpayers are 'entitled to expect high quality services'. Further, 'public services must give value for money'. 'Accountability' is presumably linked to quality in that the failure to provide services of appropriate quality will lead to complaints by the public and some form of compensation. The casual use of terms such as 'quality' and 'accountability' is somewhat unfortunate. These are terms with a variety of different meanings and deserve to be used with some precision. The generous interpreter of the way they are used in the Charter would, however, acknowledge that they are used in a way that is perfectly compatible with the government's view of the citizen as a consumer or purchaser of services. Such an interpretation ignores the fact that this is not the only relationship that the citizen has with the state.

It is not unusual for government papers to use language in a way that permits more than one interpretation. However, this White Paper is not intended to have a limited circulation among *cognoscenti* familiar with the way in which government works; its proposals are intended to have a major impact on the public who are surely entitled to know what the government's precise intentions are. If phrases such as 'giving more power to the people' are to be used then the public have a right to know what this really means. Some clues as to the government's real intentions regarding accountability may be found by an examination of one of the more frequently used terms in the Charter – 'quality'.

Walsh, in an article examining the concept of quality in public services, suggests that it has two elements (Walsh, 1991, p. 503). One of these concerns the extent to which a particular service or product conforms to its specifications. Walsh suggests that 'this is a view of quality based upon identifiable faults, which can be discovered by inspection' (Walsh, 1991, p. 504). He argues that this is a relatively static view of quality and a more dynamic perspective would consider the extent to which a product is fit for the purpose for which it is intended. Clearly, in the case of public services there is room for much debate about whether or not particular services continue to fit the purpose for which they were originally intended or indeed whether their purposes have now changed or ought to change. It might be argued that the Charter recognizes this since its introduction indicates that people should be consulted about the services they use. The Charter also recognizes the need for openness in the way services are run, their costs, the people who are responsible for operating them, and the extent to which they are meeting their standards. In order to achieve the last of these, targets are to be published, together with 'full and accurate information about results achieved' (Cabinet Office, 1991, p. 5). This may be useful in a situation where competition exists but surely has no more than informational value in monopoly situations. Information indicating the number of trains that arrive on time on a particular route says nothing about the *quality* of comfort on the journey, nor about the frequency of the service or whether the service is provided in an efficient, effective (or courteous) manner.

Walsh also cites Nelson's distinction between search goods and experience goods (Walsh, 1991, p. 504). The former can be investigated by the consumer to determine the suitability of goods or a service before it is purchased; goods and services falling into the latter category cannot be examined in advance and can only be evaluated by experience. Walsh notes that experience goods are much more likely to be evaluated in terms of their fitness for the purposes for which they are designed. Finally, he suggests that all goods combine both search and experience elements and that an examination of their suitability for any purpose is ultimately a matter of personal judgement (Walsh, 1991, p. 505).

In spite of the rhetoric about choice, most of the goods provided by the government must be seen primarily as experience goods, and this is reflected in the government's attitude towards measuring the value of such goods. A lot of emphasis is paid to the publication of performance targets. They are presumably intended to inform the citizen about the quality of goods on offer. However, there are three problems with this. The first is that the citizen may not have a choice in the services he or she receives. Indicating the number of dustbins that a contractor clears in a day does not give the local taxpayer any greater opportunity to influence who will clear his dustbins. Secondly, performance indicators give only a partial indicator of the potential effectiveness of a service. Information about the number of external examination successes of a school offers only a partial indicator of its worth as an educational establishment for a particular pupil. The style of learning encouraged by teaching staff, or the social contacts that are made may be just as important in the educational development of a pupil. Finally, it is the government that chooses the indicators rather than the citizen and clearly there may be disagreement over the choice of indicators.

Many public goods therefore cannot be fully regarded as search goods and it would be disingenuous for the government to suggest otherwise. A more effective means of ensuring fitness for use (i.e. quality) might come by permitting greater customer participation in the development of services. This raises two questions; first, who is the customer and second, how may effective customer participation be encouraged?

Since public services are funded collectively through taxation it seems strange to regard the consumer of services as the only person with an interest in the way they are delivered. Services provided by collective funding are surely bought by a number of people who have no need to consume the services but are pleased for others to do so. Such people are as much customers of the service provider as those who actually consume the service. If consumers of services were the only people with a stake in the way services are delivered then, presumably, there would be increased pressure to improve services which could result in limitless demands on those who provide funding for those services. Decisions about the quality of provision of a service must therefore result from the interaction of a variety of stakeholders, including those who consume the service, those who fund it and those who directly provide it. This has implications for the kind of information that is made available by the government and for the way it is disseminated. An attitude towards openness that relies solely on the views of consumers will be somewhat limited.

The lack of real commitment to enhancing the power of the citizen is reflected in the provision made for redress if appropriate services are not received. Where performance falls below published standards the Charter suggests that compensation should be offered to affected customers. The mechanism has well established antecedents in British government and, for example, quite closely reflects the principles behind the establishment of the Parliamentary Commissioner for Administration in 1967. It is a tradition that has been utilized in a number of areas including banking and insurance and in the watchdog bodies of privatized industries. The difference from longer established tradition is that instead of the citizen having to complain to a neutral official (for example, the Parliamentary Commissioner) in order to discover whether there is a justified case, he or she can establish this for himself by reference to a set of published criteria. However, like the Parliamentary Commissioner, the powers of citizens in relation to redress are relatively limited in the sense that they have no power to *demand* compensation and are entirely reliant on the department to determine the amount of any compensation paid. This is not a tradition that transfers any real power to the citizen, certainly not in a way which allows the citizen to participate in decisions about the nature of the service. In its own way this means that only a limited amount of information about a service needs to be released to the public (only that relating to service performance).

It is, perhaps, not surprising that the principles of redress are inadequate. One of the contradictions of the Charter is that it is based upon premises derived from the private sector and thus treats citizens as consumers of services which they do not own. However, the services covered by the Charter are precisely those that citizens do own – such as health care, transport, or the range of services provided by local authorities. A key element in the policies pursued by successive Conservative administrations in the 1980s has been to emphasize, by delegation, the need for services (especially those provided by local government) to be responsive to the wishes of its citizens. It is therefore a little strange that a Charter claiming to give more power to the individual ignores this important aspect of their citizenship.

The difficulties of ensuring effective redress form a background to the second question: how can effective public participation be encouraged? The Charter makes no specific provision for public involvement in helping to set appropriate standards or influencing the way in which services are delivered. This is implied in the Charter but its logic is not fully developed. The language used is similar to that of the Skeffington Committee in its report *People and Planning* (Ministry of Housing and Local Government, 1969), which referred to the public's right to know whether their representations had been successful or why they might not have been. This misses the point about public involvement in the provision of services. Unless the public can be confident that their views stand a good chance of being accepted, they are likely to become disillusioned by any attempt at 'consultation'.

As noted earlier, the introduction to the Charter states that one of its purposes is to give more power to the citizen. However, empowerment involves a transfer of power – the only way in which the public can receive more power is if the government, or an agency acting on its behalf, chooses to relinquish some of its powers; to adjust, as it were, the power relationship between government and the governed. The problem with the Citizen's Charter is that it implies both that the government is in some way divorced from the delivery of services and is therefore not responsible for them and also that the power of the citizen in relation to these services can be increased without this affecting the existing powers of the government. However, ultimate responsibility for the delivery of public services does lie with government (central or local) and changes that ignore this are likely to achieve very little. The Charter thus runs the risk of being a limited exercise which possibly affects the rights of individual citizens at the margin but makes no real difference to the way in which services are delivered or received.

Sherry Arnstein (1971) has set this out quite clearly in her eight-stage ladder of participation. Real citizen power lies either with citizen control of services, with delegated power or in a partnership with officials. Consultation, and the right to receive information, are only degrees of tokenism in participation and imply little transfer of power. Thus the right to be told why a train is running late, or why a hospital appointment has been cancelled reflects a pleasing sign of courtesy on the part of British Rail or a particular hospital but does nothing to increase the power of the citizen. Rights do not give citizens an opportunity of contributing to a discussion on the way in which the local hospital carries out its obligation to the local community, still less any means of contributing effectively to a discussion of what those obligations should be. In this situation there has been little real increase in power for the average citizen.

Power can be exercised in a variety of ways. One of the most important is through the dissemination of information. This is not merely a question of ensuring that information is available, but ensuring that the right information is available to increase the power of the citizen. This involves making it available in a place where it is readily accessible and in a form that allows the citizen to use it effectively. In practice, this may be difficult. Medical information, for example, is not usually available in a form that can be easily used. The rights of a patient (usually in a powerless situation anyway) are dependent upon information given by medical staff. The patient can, at best, only ask general questions of such professionals. In the light of such information the patient only rarely has any choice over medical treatment, other than to accept it or to reject it. It is an unusual patient who knows when the information received is based on evidence capable of more than one interpretation. In most cases, therefore, the patient is unable to challenge the information given. In that sense, medical advice is provided by monopolists. A charter may improve the way the monopoly is run but will not change the fact that it is a monopoly. In this case the provision of more information is unlikely to be helpful to the citizen and a significant increase in citizens' rights therefore appears unlikely.

This raises questions about the value of the Charter's approach to openness. The introduction to the Charter makes the categorical, if somewhat vague, commitment that 'there should be no secrecy about how public services are run and how much they cost' (Cabinet Office, 1991, p. 5). The principal purpose of such a statement must surely be more than justifying the publication of targets or the wearing of name tags by civil servants. If the government is serious in its stated intention to give people 'more say in the way services are run', then all aspects of the work of government should be open for examination. Further, such a statement implies rather more than merely permitting redress of grievances for those few parts of a service that the citizen directly encounters.

The express intentions of the Charter were reflected in the justifications presented for the 1993 White Paper on open government. This claimed that greater openness under the Citizen's Charter was already leading to better service for the citizen (Cabinet Office, 1993, p. 1). It went on to argue (in an attempt to justify this claim) that more information was being provided about services, that performance standards were now being published and that league tables (for example, of school examination successes) now existed to enable more informed choices to be made. Such tables, according to the White Paper, provide a stimulus to competition, choice, and service improvement (Cabinet Office, 1993, p. 1). Such information is interesting and may be useful as a basis for individual decision-making in line with the assumptions of a private Citizen's Charter. To some extent, however, it merely regularizes the availability of information that was previously broadly available. Further (as suggested earlier) some of the information may have only limited value for the purpose of influencing the decisions of policy-makers. At the same time, it must be acknowledged that some information has been useful; for example, the publication of more information on food safety and consumer protection issues.

The Code of Practice agreed after the publication of the White Paper suggests that more information could be made available in three broad areas. First, 'the facts and analyses of the facts that the Government considers relevant and important in framing major policy proposals' could be made available. Secondly, explanatory material, including a department's internal guidance on dealing with the public, could come into the public domain. Thirdly, explanations could be offered, to those affected, of the reasons for particular administrative decisions (Cabinet Office, 1994, pp. 1–2). However, the White Paper makes clear that whilst information will be made available this did not mean that the documents themselves would be produced for public scrutiny and argues, somewhat lamely, that this was because people would find it easier to ask for information rather than particular documents. This may be true, but it clearly implies that unless citizens are aware of exactly what information they want, they will not get it. In other words, there will be no possibility of trawling through a range of documents in order to find exactly what it is that one wants to know. It is perhaps unhelpful, also, that the government decided that it would not have a central strategy to implement the provisions of its code; it was left up to departments to decide what their strategy would be, subject to monitoring by the Office of Public Service and Science (now the Office for Public Policy).

Whilst the Code of Practice is undoubtedly an improvement on the situation that previously existed, it hardly marks a major advance in the direction of open government. Further, as Maurice Frankel has pointed out, the response from the public has been less than overwhelming (Frankel, 1995,

p. 17). One obvious reason for this is the lack of publicity about its existence. For all its enthusiasm for empowering the citizen, the government appears curiously unaware of the truism that unless the public are aware of the means by which they are empowered they will be unable to take advantage of it. Frankel points to the fact that, in any case, the code only covers a limited number of public functions – in essence, those already subject to scrutiny by the Ombudsman. By definition, large numbers of public issues that might be of interest to citizens fall outside the provisions of the code.

Just as important are the limitations placed on what can be revealed. Why, for example, does the code only permit the publication of facts and analyses of facts that the *government* considers relevant and important in framing major policy proposals? How can citizens discern why a department supported a particular policy if they do not have access to all the information made available to policy-makers – whether the government considers it relevant or not? Furthermore, without this right of information to all the information they need (never mind access to documents themselves), citizens will be unable to contribute effectively to the policy-making process. It is hard in these circumstances to escape the conclusion that the government's commitment to openness is limited to those issues it can control. A lack of public interest, and a consequent failure to utilize the provisions of the code is (perhaps) only to be expected. However, this perhaps does fit with the government's unstated intentions about the charter: it is not really intended to permit the citizen to participate in policy-making, only to provide some reassurance to the citizen as consumer that he or she has access to sufficient information to judge the effectiveness of services. In making such judgements the citizen must allow the government to define what is meant by effectiveness and the means by which it may be judged.

In criticizing the government's approach, however, one must be aware of the practical difficulties of extending citizen participation in the decision-making process. Openness without the capacity to contribute to the way services are run might be meaningless but raises the question of how, exactly, members of the public might be encouraged to participate. How will they fit into the decision-making process and with what effect? Since there is already a huge amount of official information available to the citizen, what reason is there to think that greater openness will automatically increase the power of the citizen? The case for open government together with associated increases in public participation in decision-making can too easily be presented in a way that implies that the policy process is rational and linear rather than messily incremental, reflecting the attempt to create a consensus from groups with competing interests (see Lindblom, 1959).

Another difficulty facing the public is what Bachrach and Baratz have termed 'the mobilization of bias', the 'set of predominant values, beliefs, rituals and institutional procedures' which operate to the advantage of some groups in the political system and to the disadvantage of others (Bachrach and Baratz, 1970, p. 8). This mobilization of bias means not only that power is distributed unequally but so too is information. Much of this information is not secret, as such, but is not revealed simply because there is no reason for it to be revealed. Further, the information will appear in certain forms, probably reflecting the interests of the producer groups who are the principal users of information. Some of it may not even appear at all if it forms part of an assumed core of knowledge shared by producers. This is one of the most difficult aspects of openness for those who do not share the values and assumptions of providers of services. How do they gain entry to a process of decision-making that is not effectively structured to permit such participation when they have difficulty in knowing which parts of the process and which issues might be susceptible to pressure from external sources? There is little point in assuming that all parts of a policy-making process are always open to external pressure. Any actor in the political process must be aware of the importance of timing, and timing (as in dramatic productions) is dependent on the way in which other actors are playing their parts. To pursue this analogy further, to take an effective part in a production one has either to be on the stage or to be ready to step from the wings when an unscripted opportunity arises. This is a time-consuming process involving a considerable knowledge of the roles that other actors are playing. Most members of the public are not in an appropriate situation to exert such influence.

A further difficulty for the consumer lies in understanding the boundary between opinion and fact. This boundary may be constantly changing; it may in itself be a matter of opinion. If professionals are uncertain about the precise location of the boundary there is obviously little chance of the consumer of services being able to do so. However, without this information, the citizen's ability to contribute to the development of policy is clearly restricted. In any case, faced with well informed officials, members of the public are likely to experience difficulties in making their views known. Finally, the change of emphasis from collective enjoyment of services to the individual purchase of services hardly increases the power of the citizen. Faced with a large bureaucracy, the individual is less likely to be able to exert influence than he or she might do as a member of a group.

There are other problems with public involvement. One concerns the public's lack of interest in issues that affect them. Arguably, they only become concerned when services are not provided as expected or when the activities of a government department effectively threaten their existing way of life. For them the provisions of the Charter may be an adequate form of political involvement. Furthermore, an increased ability to effectively challenge the activities of a department and to obtain redress of a legitimate grievance may represent a considerable extension of their direct political power. However, such an extension still leaves the individual with only limited and reactive powers in relation to the government and the bureaucracy. For the government to ignore the implications of this might be regarded as cynical. It at least ignores the possibility that the extension of power to the citizen might ignite a demand for greater powers. The only way to prevent that would be to ensure that the powers made available in the Charter are so limited that citizens are disinclined to seek to use further powers.

It is unfortunate that the Charter offers increased power over public services only in relation to faults in the services provided. Real power lies in helping to devise services which meet the requirements of members of the public. But for this, as the Skeffington Report noted in relation to planning, the public need to be educated about the nature of the services they are receiving and about the way in which policies are made. In short, they need a wider political education. This may involve different ways of making information available since the mere publication of information is not in itself a way of increasing public participation. The majority of people are informed by news brought to them second or third hand, and inevitably this has already been condensed and interpreted before it reaches them. An ever increasing stream of White Papers, Parliamentary Papers and departmental reports goes largely unread. The government might be surprised, for example, to find how many people have not read the Citizen's Charter itself. Even fewer will have analysed its contents or contributed to a debate on its usefulness. In a wider sense the public need to be taught how to use the information available to them and to know where to seek additional information where this seems necessary. Just as importantly, they need to feel that the provision of more information will increase their powers in relation to public bureaucracies. This means as much as anything a cultural change in the attitude of the British public towards those with political and administrative power. To the extent that the Charter attempts to change this culture it may be viewed as a welcome, if limited, first step. However, the provision of collective services surely involves responsibilities that go beyond the mere acceptance or rejection of whatever is supplied. A real cultural change would be to develop a belief in people's rights to be involved in determining services.

Most members of the public have a variety of other demands on their time and successive attempts at involving them in decision-making have not proved wildly successful. The lesson from this is not that citizens are apathetic or even uninterested in government but that they fail to see its relevance to them and lack the power to influence its activities.

Conclusion

It would be wrong to belittle the intentions of the Charter; improvements in services are always to be welcomed and some of the anticipated benefits will be worth waiting for, if they can be achieved. But they hardly mark a major transfer of power to the citizen. All of the expected achievements are perfectly compatible with a model of government that retains real power in the hands of senior public officials and politicians. This is hardly surprising since the issue of the transfer of power is not seriously addressed in the Charter. Nor, except at a relatively simplistic level, is the issue of openness; all that is proposed is the publication of more performance targets which the public may be able to use to assess services but which they will have played no part in determining.

The Charter only addresses one of the roles of a citizen, that of a consumer of services. However, this chapter has argued that a citizen plays more than one role in relation to the state and that these roles are inter-linked. If citizens wish to examine services provided on their behalf (over which, in a democracy, they should have some control), then they need rather more than simply information about services already provided and a (limited) ability to obtain redress whenever things go wrong. Citizens need to be able to ensure that the problems that have occurred will not happen again. Thus they need more information about the way the services operate and the opportunity to comment on this.

This logic, which points in the direction of open government, also has its difficulties. It is very difficult to find mechanisms that allow people to participate effectively in this process. The assumption of the Charter is that the prospect of public pressure will be a major determinant in making services more efficient. But public services are administered by complex organizations which are affected by their environment in a myriad of different ways. The public represent only one part of this environment and, in any particular situation, not necessarily the most important part.

Further, the redress of faults found in services is offered principally at the lowest level of the hierarchy – this ignores the possibility that problems derive from the way the organization is structured and not from the way lower-level operatives deliver the service. To that extent, the Charter ignores the fact that ultimate responsibility for the delivery of public services rests with the minister in charge of the department (or, as the case may be, with the local council). Finally, the charter fails to acknowledge the fact that improvements to service delivery may prove expensive. There is nothing in the Charter, nor in the Prime Minister's speech to the House of Commons when he introduced it, to suggest that money will be made available to help improve services should this be necessary. Indeed, there is every indication from ministerial responses to parliamentary questions that the government intends that improvements to services should be met from existing resources so that they can claim the citizen is getting increased value for money.

The Charter may therefore mark the beginning of a mechanism for improving public services but it leaves a number of questions unanswered, particularly in terms of the ability of citizens to affect the way in which services can be improved. Such questions need to be resolved if the Charter is to have an effective impact upon public services rather than proving to be an ill considered good idea. Such a lack of consideration does nothing to improve public confidence in public services.

References

Arnstein, S. (1971), 'A Ladder of Citizen Participation in the USA', *Journal of the Town Planning Institute*, April, pp. 176–82.

Bachrach, P. and Baratz, M. S. (1970), *Power and Poverty Theory and Practice*, Oxford University Press, Oxford.

Cabinet Office (1991), *The Citizen's Charter, Raising the Standard*, Cm 1599, HMSO, London.

Cabinet Office (1993), *Open Government*, Cm 2290, HMSO, London.

Cabinet Office (1994), *Code of Practice on Access to Government Information*, HMSO, London.

Frankel, M. (1995), 'State's Open Secrets', *Guardian*, 24 January, p. 17.

Lindblom, C. (1959), 'The Science of Muddling Through', *Public Administration Review*, Spring, pp. 79–88.

Ministry of Housing and Local Government (1969), *People and Planning: Report of the Committee on Public Participation in Planning* (Chairman Arthur Skeffington), HMSO, London.

Walsh, K. (1991), 'Quality and Public Services', *Public Administration*, Winter, pp. 503–514.

6 The Citizen's Charter and Quality Management: Harmony or Discord?

D. S. MORRIS AND R. H. HAIGH

Described as Premier John Major's 'big idea' – the Citizen's Charter was intended to enhance the quality of service provision within the not-for-profit organization of the public sector. However, the originality of that initiative may be questioned as its antecedents can be found in the profound changes which public sector organizations experienced from 1979 onwards. Those changes marked a clear departure from the role previously assigned to the public sector.

With the notable exception of the United States, the end of the Second World War saw both victors and vanquished sharing a similar fate: impoverishment. Whilst conceding that such a fate did not result in equal misery, it has to be recognized that it did result in equal need, namely, the rebuilding of the war-damaged European economies. Throughout postwar Europe, there appeared to be agreement among governments that re-building would require the efforts of both governmental and private capital as the task which confronted their respective societies was one that was beyond both the capacity and capability of either sector, operating in isolation, to achieve. Hence, mixed economies became the norm and the goal became collectivist endeavours in pursuit of the attainment of a common, shared goal. Later this was to be transformed into the pursuit of trans-national, European goals, through the partial surrender of sovereignty to the supra-national institutions of the European Union. Initially, however, a panacea for the ills of the separate European nations was thought by governments to reside in three main elements which were to serve as the focus for governmental policy, namely, the role of the state in economic affairs, the state provision of welfare and corporatism (see Savage and Robins, 1990).

The role of the state in economic affairs

Here the contention is that, certainly for the first two-and-a-half decades after the restoration of peace to Europe, there was widespread acceptance in Britain of the fact that the role of central government was to be a key player in the management of the economy and that the favoured form of economy was perceived to be the 'mixed economy', incorporating both private and public sector organizations. Over time, these perceptions entailed the acceptance of a number of differing forms of amalgamation of those two types of enterprise and permitted state ownership of particular parts of the economy. Government subsidies were granted to discrete industries when it was expedient so to do and included the taking of specific measures such as control over prices, incomes and credit. The rationale that underpinned all of these measures was the expressed intention of both Labour and Conservative administrations to maintain full employment. This latter objective had, of necessity, arisen because of the manifest acceptance by governments of significant elements in Keynesian economic theory, with its advocacy that government should play the role of partner to the private sector of the economy. That partnership role entailed not seeking to do that which the private sector already did, but lay in the ability of government to supplement the role of the private sector by undertaking those necessary functions which, because of commercial or other considerations, the private sector did not, would not, or could not perform.

Hence, the role of the state in the management of the British economy became twofold: first, that of changing or amending the part played by the dominant economic forces in society whilst, secondly, protecting those dominant forces and ensuring their continuance.

The role of the state in welfare provision

In Britain and throughout much of postwar Western Europe, governments expressed agreement with the contention that not only should there be welfare provision but also that government should play an active role in securing that provision. Differences lay in the extent to which state provision was countenanced and not in state provision *per se*; this explains the differing levels of state sponsored welfare provision which emerged throughout Europe in the post-war period. In Britain, both Labour and Conservative administrations accepted that the state should play a central role in the provision of welfare. They concurred that health care, income support, personal social services, care for the elderly, for children, the disabled and the homeless should be provided by government in any democratic and humane society. Such a consensus led to policies that gave the state an active part in the spheres of education, housing, pensions and social security. However, the state did not have an exclusive role, for state provision existed alongside other agents which offered services compatible with, and parallel to, state provision in all of those policy areas, while voluntary organizations also played a part in the totality of provision. What distinguished the major British political parties was the degree of contribution which they saw as being appropriate for the state and the private sector respectively to make, and not the question as to whether or not it was proper and appropriate for the state to perform and fulfil a wider function in response to societal needs.

Corporatism

Throughout the immediate post-war years, the need to rebuild or rejuvenate the economies of Western Europe led governments to utilize an approach to decision-making that in turn led to the development of a consultative climate over a broad spectrum of policy areas: ranging from economic policy through to the more specific areas of health provision and industrial policy. Britain did not prove to be an exception to this general trend. This meant that, on any particular policy question, governments sought the views and opinions of interest groups which possessed specialized knowledge of the relevant policy area during the formulation of policy and, not infrequently, the active support of those interest groups in the implementation of policy once it had been enacted. The rationale underpinning this approach was the belief that efficiency and effectiveness could best be achieved through policies which enjoyed the widest possible level of acceptance and support from among those most intimately involved in the area to which the policy was to apply. In the field of industrial policy, for example, this corporatist approach led to the development of 'tripartism'; the creation of a forum in which government and the two sides of industry, management and labour, sat down together at the same table to negotiate. The compromises, which were the inevitable outcome of the corporatist approach, were seen as being preferable to the potential conflict which might otherwise have arisen; for confrontation was perceived to hinder the attainment of the desired goals of efficiency, effectiveness and economy.

Such a scenario, which held sway through most of Western Europe for the greater part of the first three decades after the end of the Second World War, was subject to radical revision in Britain from the mid-1970s onwards. A plethora of factors can be said to have contributed to this transformation, among which would have to be included: the first oil shock of 1963; the ever-increasing cost of state provision; and the challenges presented to the British economy, particularly to its manufacturing base, by the rapid emergence and growth of the economies of its European partners, of Japan and of the 'Five Tigers' of the Pacific Rim. There was also the growing acceptance, especially in governmental circles, that Keynesian economic theory could no longer provide a solution to the problem of stagflation and that a new economic doctrine was needed to break out of the downward spiral of incipient economic decline.

The response that emerged in the late 1970s, developed in the 1980s and is still evidenced today, although now being expressed with less conviction than previously, challenged earlier thinking by questioning, from a neoliberalist perspective, the role to be played by the state in the affairs of the nation. Three new elements, the primacy of the market, individualism, and strong, if minimalist, government, came to replace those that had formerly characterized the policy-making process.

The primacy of the market

The virtues of the market were to reign supreme in economic affairs, a view typified by Prime Minister Thatcher's assertion that 'you cannot buck the market'. The role of the state in the management of the mixed economy was replaced by conviction that the market was the best mechanism for the efficient, effective and economical distribution of finite resources. The supremacy of the market over state-run or state-directed enterprises in all sectors of the economy was proclaimed; with the former being viewed as the means through which economic rejuvenation could best be facilitated and secured, whilst the latter, isolated from market forces and artificially protected from competition, were claimed to be characterized by inefficiency and ineffectiveness and sustained only through extensive and ever-growing financial support from government. The acceptance of neo-liberal principles provided the ideological justification for the government to commence the task of 'rolling back the frontiers of the state' in the economic and social life of the nation and for the encouragement of competition in the public sector. In Britain, for example, compulsory competitive tendering for previously publicly run services, market testing, hiving-off and privatization of wholly state-owned assets became the norm. Such actions were incompatible with Keynesian economic theory which had for so long provided an accepted basis for the management of the economy, and in its place were paraded the more avowedly microeconomic and monetarist doctrines of Hayek and Friedman.

Strong government

At first glance this might appear to stand in marked contrast with a reduced role for the state, but a closer examination serves to show that, at least in the short term, strong government is a prerequisite for ensuring a departure from former patterns. Only strong government, it was contended, could free the economy from the constricting web of state regulation which was seen to have imposed unwanted and unwarranted limitations upon the development of an enterprise culture. Only a strong government could cut through the constraints imposed upon private and public enterprises by trade unions, which were viewed as having become too powerful and which were able to restrict 'the right of mangers to manage'. Only a strong government would suffice to oblige the citizenry to recapture its former initiative, self-respect and self-reliance and ensure the attainment of national prosperity. In the eyes of successive Conservative administrations, only strong government could ensure that its efforts on all of these fronts would not be undermined by increasing European integration, by the threat that was seen to be posed to British national interests by those arguing for a federal Europe and by the 'creeping socialism' associated, by his opponents, with Jacques Delors.

Inevitably, such changed policy orientations impacted upon the organizations of the public sector. At the most general level they have presented a challenge to those who would contend that public sector organizations are characterized by certain unique features which clearly distinguish them from their counterparts in the private sector; features such as:

- they are not exposed to the competitive world of the market;

- their objectives are usually ill defined and expressed only in vague terms; terms such as 'serving the public';
- short-term considerations make it difficult for them to engage in strategic planning;
- they are susceptible to greater and more open accountability;
- their functions are limited by statute;
- they are funded from taxation and not by charging the market price for their products and services;
- certain services can only be provided by the state and such services cannot be left to the vagaries of market forces for, if such were to be the case, those services would not be provided (Lawton and Rose, 1991).

Contrasting with the 'unique public sector' is the argument that its distinguishing features have indeed lost their uniqueness. This argument contends that, over the last two decades, a convergence has been taking place between the public and private sector with the result that:

- increasingly, the organizations of the public sector charge for some of the services which they offer;
- the private sector increasingly operates within an environment in which government policy and decisions have a direct impact upon its actions;
- constraints imposed by statute are also a feature of the private sector;
- joint public and private schemes and programmes are a feature of certain areas of activity (Lawton and Rose, 1991).

When the convergence argument is coupled with the assumption that private management equates with good and that public management equates with bad and when it is further contended that generic management is not a hypothesis but a reality, the opportunity is present for a change in the style of management within public sector organizations; a change that is compatible with the more far-reaching changed orientation of the role of the public sector itself.

In practice, what has emerged is a changed 'way of doing things and of getting things done' in public sector organization. This transformation may be characterized as a movement from public services that were formerly administered to public services that are now to be managed. The contrast between administration and management is outlined in Figure 6.1.

It is against the foregoing background that the Citizen's Charter has to be considered. In essence, the Charter proposes seven principles which are

	Administration	Management
Goals	In general terms, infrequently reviewed or changed	Broad strategic aims, supported by more detailed short-term goals and targets
Attainment criteria	Mistake avoiding	Success seeking
Resource use	Secondary task	Primary task
Organizational structure	Roles defined in terms of responsibility Long hierarchies Limited delegation	Roles defined in terms of tasks Shorter hierarchies Maximum delegation
Management role	Arbitrator	Protagonist
Perceptions	Passive: workload determined outside system. Best people used to solve problems Time insensitive Risk avoiding Emphasis on procedure Conformity to national standards	Active: seeking to influence environment. Best people used to discover and exploit opportunities Time sensitive Risk accepting but minimalizing Emphasis upon results Local experiments: need for conformity to be proved
Skills	Legal and quasi-legal Literacy	Economic/socio-economic Numeracy

Figure 6.1 A comparison between administration and management

intended to clarify and, ultimately, to enhance the standard of service which public sector organizations provide to their users, the customers:

- standards: explicit statements covering employee behaviour and levels of service which should be prominently displayed;
- openness: about how public services are run, how much they cost and whether they are meeting the standards which have been set;
- information: full and accurate information in plain language which can be understood by the user;
- choice: public consultation should take place and choice be offered wherever possible;
- non-discrimination: services should be available irrespective of race or sex;
- accessibility: services should be run to suit the convenience of customers;
- redress: a well-publicized and readily available complaints procedure.

Therefore, it would appear that what is being sought through the introduction of the Charter is to make public sector organizations more responsive to customer needs by treating the users as customers and by endowing those customers with the entitlements which they hold in their dealings with private sector organizations. This endeavour, to portray the end user as a customer, is compatible with the attempts to introduce private sector management practices into public sector organizations and to ensure compatibility with the movement from administration to management which has been established in the public sector.

As with other attempts to encourage the adoption of private sector managerial practices in public sector organizations, the Charter has been imposed from outside those organizations by the government. The specific details relating to the level of provision made by a service or organization have been formulated by various representative and non-representative bodies. The details of the standards to which services will be provided have been determined not by the customer but on behalf of the customer and so have been delineated in the light of those bodies' own priorities and political agendas. Despite the rhetoric of the Charter, in essence, the end user has not been treated as a customer but as a consumer, simply because the majority of public service provision is free at the point of delivery.

What has emerged from the Charter are standards of public service quality which are deemed by the providers of public services to be appropriate to meet the needs of, essentially, non-directly paying consumers rather than the needs of paying customers. In the case of the former, quality is determined for the end user, the consumer. In the case of the latter, quality is determined by the end user, the customer. In short, therefore, despite the protestations to the contrary, the Charter is not about 'quality', for quality can only be determined by the end user as customer and must accord with a universally accepted definition of quality as fitness for customers' usage; a definition that demands that the determination of quality resides not with the supplier of a product or service but with the user of that product or service.

In addition, there is the issue of the extent to which the satisfaction of customer needs is the central force underpinning the corporate provision of a product or service. The Charter, by accepting the necessity to recognize the need to redress grievance, clearly lays the emphasis upon the public service to detect and acknowledge failure to deliver a standard of service that is deemed by the end users, the consumers, to meet their needs. Quality management would contend that the prevention of the failure to meet the needs of end users is the essence of the provision of a quality service.

The essential difference which may be detected between the Charter and the tenets of quality management resides in the difference between detection of failure to meet a supplier-set standard of provision to consumers and offering to customers a standard of service provision that meets their expressed needs. Therefore, the difference is between having a philosophy of service provision that is supplier-determined and driven, as opposed to a philosophy of service provision that is customer-driven and towards which all corporate actions are orientated. In that difference resides the distinction between a piecemeal philosophy towards quality and a *weltanschauung* philosophy toward the attainment of quality.

This contention may be discerned and supported through a consideration of the philosophy that underpins quality management. Elsewhere we have sought to delineate the parameters of the philosophy that is the rationale for TQM (see, for example, Kanji et al., 1993). In essence, we have argued that TQM, in common with all philosophies, be they political, social or economic, contains four constant, core elements: a challenge to the status quo, a set of values, a vehicle for change, and a specification of the future desired state that is being sought:

- *a challenge to the status quo*: a critique of the past and present. Lowe and McBean (1989) cogently represent the deficiencies in current management practice in both the manufacturing and service sectors of western economies. They choose to do so through a detailed analysis of four key managerial indicators, namely, management beliefs, management practices, management systems and processes and people attitudes (see Figure 6.2).

- *Set of values*: which serve as the cement that binds the components of the philosophy together and which further provides it with coherence and sustains its advocacy, adoption and implementation. Here both the manufacturing and service sectors of the economy are favoured by the work of Parasuraman et al. 1985, who provide a comprehensive coverage of the expectations that customers entertain of any enterprise to exhibit in their interactions with it:
- *Access*: involves *approachability* and *ease* of contact.
- *Communication*: means keeping the customers *informed*, in language that they can understand, and *listening* to them.

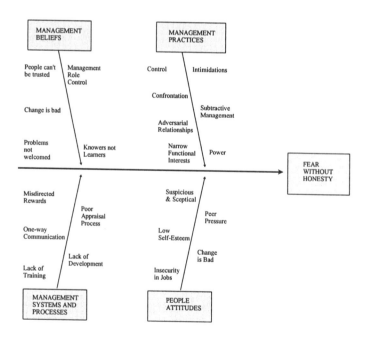

Figure 6.2   An analysis of four key managerial indicators (after Lowe and McBean, 1989)

- *Competence*: means possession by the organization's personnel of the required skills and knowledge to perform the service or deliver the organization's product.
- *Courtesy*: includes politeness, respect, consideration and friendliness of the organization's personnel.
- *Reliability*: involves consistency of performance and dependability.
- *Responsiveness*: involves the willingness, readiness and timeliness of employees to provide service or product.
- *Security*: is freedom from danger, risk and doubt.[1]
- *Tangibles*: include the physical evidence of the quality of service provision or product efficacy.
- *Understanding/knowing the customer*: involves making the effort to understand the customers' needs and expectations.
- *A vehicle for change*: TQM, through its effective implementation, is perceived as the vehicle for change which will sweep away the old management practices characteristic of the status quo and herald the dawn of a new era of effective management. Whilst the quality gurus may differ in their prescriptions for the implementation of TQM, there is sufficient of a consensus for it to be possible to discern a number of agreed features of TQM that permit it to be utilized as a vehicle for change:
  - *The customer is king*: for Feigenbaum (1983), TQM '. . . start[s] with the customer's requirements and end[s] successfully only when the customer is satisfied with the way the product or service meets those requirements'.
  - *Everyone participates in TQM*: to Ishikawa (1983) this means the involvement of not just the top, senior and middle managers in the organization and its first line supervisors but the entire workforce and, more recently, '. . . the subcontractors, distribution systems and affiliated companies'.
  - *Quality measurement is essential*: Crosby (1979) is insistent and clear that 'quality measurements for each area of activity must be established where they don't exist and reviewed where they do'.
  - *Align corporate systems to support quality*: Imai (1986) makes it manifest that where '. . . existing systems and corporate structures . . . are found inappropriate for meeting cross functional goals . . . necessary changes (must be made)'.
  - *Constantly strive for quality improvement*: Deming (1986) instructs that we must 'improve constantly and forever the system of

production and service, to improve quality and productivity, and thus to constantly decrease costs'.

- *A future desired state*: in which the past and current managerial practices have been eradicated and in which the new practices, secured through the active implementation of TQM, as a vehicle for change, have become endemic. That which is being actively sought can be represented diagrammatically (as in Figure 6.3).

Here it may be contended that both the Charter and TQM offer prescription but fall short of offering a mechanism through which that prescription may be made manifest in terms of action. In short, neither offers a model for implementation. Indeed, the partial nature of the tenets of the Charter and the absence of holism render the development of an implementational model virtually impossible; there is simply an inadequate philosophy presented to permit systematic implementation. However, whilst

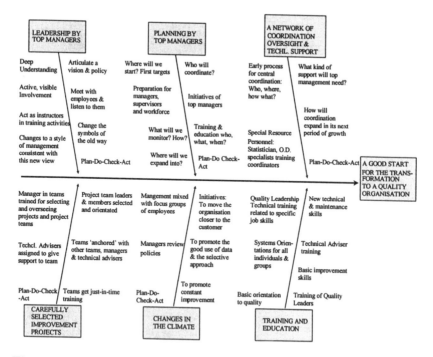

Figure 6.3 The aims of TQM

the creative gurus of TQM have failed to provide an implementational model for their prescriptions, the holistic nature of those prescriptions does afford a basis for model building which can serve as a guide to operational management.

Our intention is to offer a model that makes the underpinning philosophy of TQM capable of operationalization under existing organizational conditions.

A model for the implementation of TQM

However, at the outset, it must be recognized that there is no one type of model and that there are many traps associated with model building. Golembiewski et al. (1969) contend that we often overlook the 'simple . . . datum that there are at least two types of models, each having its own uses and liabilities'. Here we betray our initial training as political scientists and seek to illustrate this assertion by reference to the work of Rousseau. His 'Social Contract' typifies a utopian model, whilst his work 'On the Government of Poland' is reality-based. Rousseau's work illustrates also the uses and abuses of the two basic types of model. Utopian models may serve as an analytical standard against which existing practices and conditions may be compared, whilst a reality-based model exhibits the extent to which the utopian elements were achieved under actual operating conditions. Hazardously, we attempt to cross that divide between the two types of basic model by seeking to make good the deficiencies we have discerned in the work of the gurus through the development of a generic model for the implementation of TQM.

Such a model must encompass both the macro, contextual elements of TQM as well as taking cognizance of the micro, operational elements of that approach to management, the former being the responsibility of top management, the latter being the responsibility of first-line operatives with middle management playing a crucial linkage role. At the same time, it is imperative that the macro and micro elements be interconnected to provide the holism demanded by the word 'total'. With these considerations very much in mind, we offer the generic model shown in Figure 6.4.

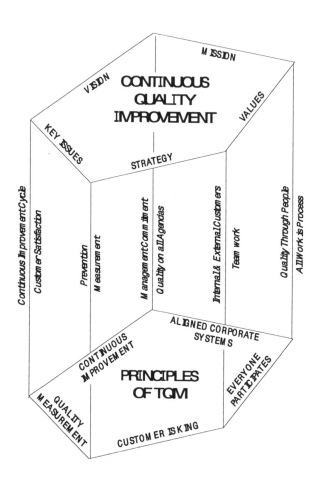

Figure 6.4   A generic model for the implementation of TQM (after Morris and Haigh, 1994)

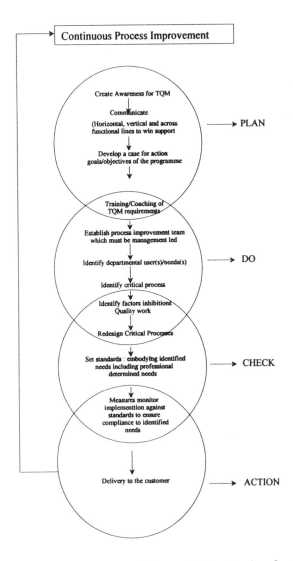

Figure 6.5   **A more specific model for the implementation of TQM (after Nwabueze et al., 1994)**

Yet even this model, whilst affording a return to the holism demanded by the philosophy that underpins TQM, does not progress much beyond a position of considerable generalization. To be of use to our practising manager it is imperative that we develop its central sections; those that link the principles of TQM with the wider contextual activities of vision, mission, strategy, values and key issues. It is these central sections that provide the basis for the day-to-day activities that make TQM manifest within an organization. To do this requires recourse to a further implementational model of greater specificity (Figure 6.5).

At this juncture it is imperative that we pose the question: 'How strong is this implementational model?'. Strictly speaking this is a question that ought to be answered by someone other than ourselves, but for now we will treat it as being a rhetorical question. We would contend that any model has to be assessed against certain criteria:

- *Validity*: this entails three elements:
  the correspondence of the model with the reality it purports to represent;
  the model's susceptibility to operationalization;
  possible errors of structural commission.
- *Flexibility*: the susceptibility of the model to changes in the number, nature or interrelatedness of its variables;
- *Generality*: the breadth of relevance of the model;
- *Significance*: the model's applicability to important problems raised by the implementation of TQM;
- *Internal Logic*: sequential compatibility between the elements of the model.

Conclusion

In conclusion, the following assessment is offered. The Citizen's Charter represents an attempt to build upon the changes that have taken place in the role of public sector organizations and upon the managerial changes that have followed in its wake. It has sought to do so by seeking to insert the voice of the end user, as consumer, into the intra-organizational decision-making processes. Yet the voice of the consumer has been heard only indirectly, even by proxy, for what is offered to the consumer is a level public service provision that is determined by the supplier of that service. In addition, the absence of a coherent philosophy to underpin service provision, designed to ensure that attention is focused upon the holistic nature of organizational endeavours, has rendered any attempt to operationalize the notions of quality contained within the Charter virtually impossible. All that can remain are partial and organizationally idiosyncratic efforts to implement, on an *ad hoc* basis, the ephemeral spirit of quality improvements in the range and level of services offered by the public sector on the basis of a supplier-determined assessment of customer needs.

By way of contrast, TQM offers not only an inherent concentration upon the needs and expectations of the end user, as customer, but ensures that customer priorities inform each and every step in the process through which a service is offered to the customer. In addition, TQM is sustained by a philosophical rationale that is, in essence, corporate both in terms of its scope and its capacity to inform operational management.

The vague notions of the needs and expectations of the customer, so very much a feature of the Charter, are substituted, in TQM, by a specific notion of quality derived from the customers' expressed needs and expectations, which are then utilized to facilitate and inform the process of service delivery.

Currently, there would appear to be little possibility of harmony between the two approaches to the delivery of enhanced public service quality and discord will remain until the Charter is taken out of the realm of political discourse and enhanced by the addition of mechanisms designed to transform vague prescription into operational reality.

Note

1. Note the contrast between negative and positive freedom; the notion of 'freedom from' as opposed to 'freedom to'. This distinction is implicit in the concept of empowerment.

References

Cabinet Office (1991), *The Citizen's Charter: Raising the Standard*, Cm 1599, HMSO, London.
Crosby, P. (1979), *Quality is Free*, McGraw Hill, New York.
Deming, W.E. (1986), *Out of Crisis*, MIT Press, Cambridge, MA.
Feigenbaum, A.V. (1983), *Total Quality Control*, 3rd edn, McGraw Hill, New York.

Golembiewski, R.T., Welsh, W.W. and Crotty, W.W. (1969), *A Methodological Primer for Political Scientists*, Rand McNally, Chicago.

Imai, M. (1986), *Kaizen: the Key to Japan's Competitive Success*, Random House, New York.

Ishikawa, K. (1983), *What is Quality Control?*, Prentice Hall, New Jersey.

Kanji, G.K., Morris, D.S. and Haigh, R.H. (1993), 'Philosophical and Systems Dimensions of Total Quality Management', in *Proceedings of the Advances in Quality Systems for TQM*, Taipei.

Keeling, D. (1972), *Management in Government*, Allen and Unwin, London.

Lawton, A. and Rose, A. (1991), *Organization and Management in the Public Sector*, Pitman, London.

Lowe, J.A. and McBean, G.M. (1989), 'Honesty without Fear', in *Proceedings of the 43rd Annual Congress of the American Society for Quality Control*, Toronto.

Morris, D.S. and Haigh, R.H. (1994), 'Achieving Process Improvements: a Case Study in the Utilization of TQM Within a College of Further Education', in *Proceedings of 4th International Conference on Teaching Statistics*, Marrakesh.

Nwabueze, U., Morris, D.S. and Haigh, R.H. (1994), 'TQM in the NHS: Impotence to Progress', in *Proceedings of the 10th International Conference of the Israel Society for Quality*, Jerusalem.

Parasuraman, A., Zeitham, I.V. and Berry, L. (1985), 'A Conceptual Model of Service Quality and its Implications for Future Research', *Journal of Marketing*, vol. 49, Fall.

Savage, S. and Robins, L. (1990), *Public Policy under Thatcher*, Macmillan, London.

7 The Patient's Charter

ANN WALL

Introduction

The Patient's Charter was published in October 1991 and, in response to criticism that it was over-concerned with hospital services, a second Charter for GP services was launched on 4 December 1992. In 1995 these were revised and amalgamated under the title 'The Patient's Charter and You' (Department of Health, 1995). A copy of the original Patient's Charter was delivered to every home in Britain at a cost of £2 million. It was concerned both with rights to health care, appearing to confirm the right to health as an essential component of citizenship, and with service standards, two issues that have lain at the heart of debate surrounding the National Health Service (NHS) since its inception in 1948. The intention in this chapter is to examine the Charter in the light of its background, the likelihood of its implementation, its potential contribution to improving service efficiency and health status; and the part it might play in enhancing citizenship.

Background to the Patient's Charter

In 1948 certain key values were enshrined in the newly-created NHS: comprehensiveness, universality, equality and the idea that services should be free at the point of use. The espousal of these values signalled the intention of the government to do more than simply provide health care. The purpose was to establish rights to health care as part of a broader package of social rights which included the right to education and a decent standard of living. It was through the forging of social rights that the concept of citizenship was to be enlarged. In this sense, the 'founding values' of the NHS were, simultaneously, the expression of the notion of citizenship and the means by which it was to be pursued.

The NHS was subsequently described as the 'very temple of our social security system' by Harold Wilson and as one of the twin pillars of the welfare state. It was the envy of the world, attracting foreign visitors, not only to avail themselves of 'free' health care, but also to observe the workings of this great social experiment. In stressing rights to health care, some forty-three years later, the Charter recalled and reaffirmed the moral foundations of the NHS.

The emphasis in the Charter on service standards reflects an on-going concern with the quality of the service which has not always lived up to the promise implied in the 'founding values'. Clearly, a detailed discussion of the reasons for this is beyond the scope of this chapter. However, in a very general sense it can be said that the NHS was beset by apparently intractable problems of soaring costs; difficulties associated with accountability, redress of grievance and entitlement; and persistent inequalities related to socio-economic status, geographic location, gender and race. Demographic, epidemiological, and technological trends in the decades which followed the war intensified rather than relieved the problems, by raising expectations and swelling demand for services. This all added weight to the argument that the NHS was a victim of its own success; its objectives were too ambitious in the context of the late twentieth century; and acceptable standards were increasingly hard to achieve.

In tackling the problems and seeking to deliver a good standard of health care to the whole population, a professional service model operated, in which standard-setting and quality were primarily matters for clinical staff, particularly the doctors. This was not self-evidently the only, or even the best, way of proceeding. It occurred because a number of factors coincided to afford the medical profession considerable power. The NHS was grounded in a curative, biomedical model of health and, therefore, those in possession of expert, scientific and increasingly esoteric knowledge inevitably held sway. The sovereign position of the doctors was sustained by the fact that other clinical occupations were far less well developed in professional terms and health service administration, described by Bosanquet (1982) as the old colonial system, was essentially reactive. It was such factors that contributed to the effectiveness of doctors as a pressure group and to the degree of respect and deference accorded them by other professionals and by the public. Medical hegemony thus flourished and doctors were able to enjoy almost unlimited freedom in the clinical domain and the ability to exert considerable influence on NHS policy.

The extent of medical power, however, was a source of unease, and both Labour and Conservative governments sought to curb it, although by different means. On the one hand, the Labour Party was concerned to promote political accountability and to place faith in democratic mechanisms as the best means of maintaining standards in health care; a strategy that resulted, in 1974, in the appointment of a Health Service Commissioner, the creation of the Health Advisory Service and community health councils; and the introduction of local authority representation on health authorities.

The Conservatives, on the other hand, since the mid-1970s, systematically strengthened the managerial constituency and this strategy produced policies of consensus and then general management, efficiency measures and, more recently, the creation of the internal market. The Charter was a predictable addition to the Conservative repertoire in that it can be seen as a move to further strengthen the hand of the managerial constituency *vis-à-vis* the medical professions in the field of setting and maintaining standards of care.

More generally, the Charter can be seen as the latest in a long line of initiatives by both major political parties designed to address the issue of quality in health care. Indeed, the Labour and Liberal Democrat parties have favoured charters, and even claim prior authorship. Taylor (1991) argued that it is hard to distinguish between Labour and Conservative proposals. In principle, at least, Labour favour citizens' as opposed to consumers' charters and stress that recognition must be given to the common interest of individuals as consumers and as citizens. The Liberal Democrats have talked more explicitly in terms of citizenship, and of fostering political rights in order to develop consumerism into citizenship. They argue that both the Labour and Conservative parties currently confuse consumerism with citizenship.

The Patient's Charter can, then, be viewed as part of a formal endorsement of the right to health care, a public statement of good practice, and an implied commitment, at least, on the part of the government to that practice. It thus appeared to offer some safeguards against further erosion and privatization, which many believe to have been on the hidden agenda during the last decade, and should, therefore, have been welcomed by those concerned with maintaining both the notion of health as a right of citizenship, and the delivery of good quality health care. Indeed, in publishing charters, and staking so much on them, John Major departed from the Conservative government's policy of shifting responsibility from the state onto individuals and families. By reaffirming that the NHS does have certain obligations to its users, the Charter, in this respect at least, belies Mrs Thatcher's claim that there is 'no such thing as society'.

The task of creating a framework within which the validity of this interpretation can be assessed proved to be treacherous. Far from being the precise, legal document it was designed to look like, the Charter is, in fact, rife with ambiguities, woolliness and unanswered questions.

There are three flaws, in particular, which made it difficult to structure a critique. The first relates to the Charter objectives which are never made explicit. The government goes no further than saying that the Charter 'is a central part of [the] programme to improve and modernize the delivery of the service to the public' (Department of Health, 1991a, p. 4). It does not specify what part it is to play or how it is to relate to other initiatives in the field of health care. Thus any suggestion that the Charter might fall short with respect to community care or health promotion, for example, can be countered by reference to other initiatives dealing with those aspects of health care. Nevertheless, the Charter is designed to improve the health service and the health service is meant to produce 'clear and measurable benefits to health' (Department of Health, 1991a, p. 5). So it is necessary to assume that the purpose of the Charter is to improve the health service and, thereby, improve the health status of the population.

A second flaw is that the status of the Charter commitments is ambiguous. By stating explicitly that the standards 'are not legal rights' (Department of Health, 1991a, p. 6), the government leaves open the question of what status they do have. Moreover, does this mean, by implication, that the rights do have a basis in law and, if so, how will they be secured? Interestingly, in the revised version of the Charter, the notion of 'expectations' was introduced and defined as the 'standards of service which the NHS is aiming to achieve. Exceptional circumstance may sometimes prevent these standards being met' (Department of Health, 1995, p. 4).

In fact, the distinction between rights and standards is never made clear in the original Charter and the blurring between the two is, if anything, more marked and deliberate in the revised version. Some of the rights incorporate standards and, conversely, some of the standards embody rights. In neither case is there an unequivocal commitment to the patient that they will be secured and consequently, the charge that patients are still waiting too long, or waiting lists have not been reduced or someone did not get a named nurse may, in fact, mean very little. However, the Charter is meaningless if the intention is not to ensure that the commitments are met. Madsen Pirie, President of the Adam Smith Institute, rightly argues that 'the success of the Charter will be won and lost in the details of its application' (*The Guardian*, 12 July 1991). However, whether the Charter is intended to be a legal contract, a pledge or a bureaucratic tool was, and remains, unclear.

A third flaw stems from the breadth of the Charter, which ranges from very broad implications for citizenship to specific recommendations regarding the maximum waiting time in an outpatient clinic. This raises the questions of whether the two extremes are consistent with one another and why the government chose to link service standards with the idea of citizenship. The answer to the first is that they are probably not and, with respect to the second question, it is likely that the government believed there was some political capital to be gained. In other words, the deliberate juxtaposing of service standards with notions of citizenship suggests a hidden agenda.

In the light of these flaws, be they accidental or otherwise, and the assumptions that have to be made as a consequence, three questions suggest themselves as a basis for analysis.

- Will the rights and standards be implemented?
- Will the implementation of the rights and standards improve health services and health status?
- Will citizenship be enhanced?

It will be argued that the Charter rights and standards are unlikely to be implemented; even where they are, this will have no more than a marginal beneficial impact on health services and health status, and may even have undesirable effects; and a Charter of this kind is an inappropriate device for the purpose of enhancing citizenship.

Content of the Charter

The Charter deals with three distinct issues:

- *rights* to health care (reaffirming 'well-established' ones within the NHS and adding three allegedly new ones relating to information, admission time and complaints);
- national and local *target standards* for service delivery which focus on waiting times and the availability and dissemination of information; and
- ways in which *monitoring of performance and progress* towards achieving the targets can be measured (Department of Health, 1991a, pp. 6–15).

Rights

The Charter begins by making reference to rights, reaffirming 'well-established' rights within the NHS, namely:

- to receive health care on the basis of clinical need regardless of ability to pay;
- to be registered with a GP;
- to receive emergency medical care at any time;
- to be referred to a consultant acceptable to you;
- to be given a clear explanation of any treatment proposed;
- to have access to your health records, and to know that those working for the NHS are under a legal duty to keep their contents confidential; and
- to choose whether or not you wish to take part in medical research or medical student training (Department of Health, 1991a, pp. 8–9).

To these it adds three allegedly new ones:

- to be given detailed information on local health services, including quality standards and maximum waiting times;
- to be guaranteed admission for treatment by a specific date no later than two years (subsequently reduced to eighteen months) from the day when your consultant places you on a waiting list;
- to have any complaint about NHS services – whoever provides them – investigated and to receive a full and prompt written reply from the chief executive or general manager (Department of Health, 1991a, pp. 10–11).

Standards

Alongside the rights to health care, the Charter makes reference to national standards which are to be achieved in nine key areas. These are:

- respect for the person;
- equality of opportunity;
- availability of information;
- waiting time for the ambulance service;
- waiting time in accident and emergency departments;
- waiting time in outpatient clinics;
- cancellation of operations;
- a named nurse; and
- discharge from hospital (Department of Health, 1991a, pp. 12–15).

The Charter then goes on to explain that local health authorities will be required to set and publicize clear local Charter standards on such matters as waiting times for first outpatient appointments and waiting times in accident and emergency departments.

As mentioned above, the basis of the distinction between rights and standards is less than crystal clear. Some of the rights, either implicitly or explicitly, incorporate standards. For example, the second of the three new rights sets a standard for waiting times in respect of inpatient admissions. Conversely, some of the standards embody rights such as, the right to privacy, information, and a named nurse. Whether the blurring is deliberate or not, it does mean that there is a lack of clarity with respect to the status of the various commitments inherent in the rights and standards.

Implementation

The Charter is much stronger on what the rights and standards are than on how they will be translated into practice. Yet it would be patently naive to believe that the Charter will be self-acting. Simply stating a right or setting a standard is not enough – even though it is very common. In the same year as the Charter was published, the government published a Green Paper and a White Paper on the health of the nation which set targets both for the reduction of the incidence of certain illnesses and for tackling some of the causes of those illnesses (Department of Health, 1991b, p. 6, 1992). Targets were also the mechanism adopted by John Major in his 'Opportunity 2000' initiative which was designed to boost women's involvement in the workforce.

Both of these programmes have been roundly criticized for failing to address the question of how the targets, having been agreed and set, are to be achieved (see, for example, O'Keefe, et al., 1992; Baggott, 1994). Yet this is a crucial aspect of the whole exercise. If the Charter rights and standards are to have any meaning, consideration must be given to how they are to be achieved and, where they are not, applying sanctions. The effectiveness of the Charter depends, to a large extent, upon the initiative being taken where a service falls short of the agreed standard.

In this context, the ambiguity surrounding the status of the Charter commitments is, again, relevant. Given that they are not legal rights, there are no legal sanctions or any mention of redress through the courts or tribunals. Indeed, attempts to use the judicial system for the purpose of establishing rights in the NHS in the past have been notoriously unsuccessful.

Where, then, does responsibility for implementation lie? The Charter is predictably vague in this regard. Clearly the government has a part to play with respect to setting the standards, and details its own responsibility in the following terms:

- to ensure the collection and publication of information (about good and bad practice); and
- to require health authorities to develop and publish local standards. (Department of Health, 1991a, p. 7)

The NHS and its staff have a general responsibility to ensure that services comply with standards. Interestingly, in the Charter, the NHS is referred to as if it were separate from the government. 'The government looks to the NHS to achieve . . . ' (Department of Health, 1991a, p. 6), thus effectively restricting its own liability. More specifically, purchasers (by and large, health authorities and GPs) will have to incorporate target standards in the contracts they let to providers.

Professional service providers continue to have a very obvious and immediate duty to deliver services that meet the target standards. They are likely, in true professional style, to demand additional resources, and these are unlikely to be forthcoming. Many commentators are unhappy on this count. The Royal College of Nursing, for example, has expressed its concern that there will be an insufficient number of qualified nurses to meet the target relating to 'named nurses'; Taylor (1991) talks of the dwindling resources and low staff morale which will confound the Charter. The government offers no reassurance, referring in the Charter to the standards it seeks to achieve 'as circumstances and resources allow' (Department of Health, 1991a, p. 6).

With respect to monitoring performance against agreed standards and imposing sanctions in the event of the commitments not being met, again, the government has certain obligations. The Charter states that 'where performance is unsatisfactory, the Secretary of State will require the Chief Executive of the NHS to take action to put things right . . . [and] The Department of Health will publish details of this action' (Department of Health, 1991a, pp. 7, 19). David Brindle suggested that failure to meet targets would be 'a severe embarrassment to the government' (*The Guardian*, 31 October 1991). However, since governments have a remarkably high embarrassment threshold, the patient is hardly likely to be reassured.

There is a suggestion, but no more, in the Charter, that the task of monitoring performance against standards will rest with the health authority which, as the purchaser, may impose sanctions on providers who fail to meet standards. Certainly, health authorities are explicitly required to publish annual performance reports. But the introduction of the internal market alone would have achieved this; it did not need a Charter. Moreover, there will be considerable scope for buck-passing between purchasers and providers.

Within both purchaser and provider organizations, the Charter hints that managers' performance pay will depend on achieving targets. Thus the Charter could be used not merely to judge the quality of the health services, but also to evaluate the performance of managers.

At the heart of the Charter is the notion of consumer 'empowerment', the idea of providing patients with a tool to use in their negotiations with service providers. The initial failure, on the part of the service, to meet standards must be noticed and acted upon by the patient. But, in the absence of any right of redress through courts or tribunals, to whom does the patient go? Significantly, where patients feel they have been denied their rights, they are encouraged to write to the NHS Chief Executive rather than to their MP. 'The . . . Charters . . . are prime examples of the government dispensing with any form of democratic control of public services in favour of "management by objectives" ' (*The Observer*, 2 July 1995). In other words, what the Charter offers is more accurately described as managerial accountability than either legal or political rights.

It is not the first time that a government has attempted to empower patients. Patients have always had a voice in the NHS and rights of redress when they are dissatisfied with the service received and experience suggests that these do not work very well. Patients and the public at large are loath to participate and reluctant to complain. Moreover, their ability and willingness to complain is related to a number of social factors such as class and ethnic background, which the Charter fails to acknowledge. Interestingly, in the original Charter no mention was made of information being available in languages other than English, or in braille or audio media; an omission rectified in the revised version. Thus, if the Charter strengthens the lay constituency at all, it will be only marginally and then only those who are white, middle class and reasonably articulate are likely to benefit.

It is tempting to argue that some of the standards have been phrased in such a way as to make enforcement very difficult. Sheffield's local Charter, for example, says: 'In outpatient clinics, you can *normally* expect to be seen within thirty minutes of your appointment time' (emphasis added). The introduction of the notion of expectations adds weight to this argument and, despite the achievements listed in the revised Charter, doubt remains that the NHS is able to fulfil the Charter promises.

Improvement in efficiency and health status

Even if the rights and standards could be guaranteed, would this have the positive impact on health status and health services implied by the Charter? In other words, can a Charter of this kind identify and address issues which are directly relevant to health and health care?

Arguably, by far the most important aspect of health care is the effectiveness of the treatment. Yet treatment cannot be the subject of a Charter. It is the most difficult part of health care to define in quantifiable terms and it is properly the remit of the professionals. Thus, it is necessarily the delivery of care rather than its substance upon which the Charter focuses. In other words, the nature of a Charter fosters an emphasis on peripheral rather than central health concerns. This distinction between core and peripheral matters is a characteristic of all professional services and is in contrast to many non-professional services. In British Rail, for example, it is possible, in a passenger's Charter, to get to the crux of what rail travellers want: an adequate number of clean, safe trains running on time. Paradoxically, because a patient's Charter cannot get to the heart of health care, the NHS could meet all the targets and still provide a poor service, and, conversely, deliver an excellent service yet fail to meet any of the targets.

Moreover, within this sphere of peripheral activities, it is the more measurable aspects such as speed, courtesy and information that will be included and less tangible but equally important matters, like time spent with a frail old person, reassuring a frightened pre-operative patient, or giving advice to a new mother that will be overlooked.

Despite the fact that Charter standards can address only part of the picture, it could still be argued that a Charter to guide and assess practice in these areas is beneficial. However, there remain a number of problems with the setting of standards.

First, the legalistic slant to the Charter is incompatible with the discretionary nature of any kind of personal service. It is not by accident that health and social care have always been organized at a local level with professional judgement playing a large part in determining what is to be done. Health care needs cannot be articulated in the precise and explicit fashion necessary for a legal contract. It is often, therefore, inappropriate to apply universal rules or impose uniform standards in these areas because of the diversity and variability of health needs which can be adequately assessed only in professional terms. Even relatively straightforward conditions such as hernias are not all the same, either in a clinical sense or in terms of their impact on the individual's life and ability to meet obligations. Hence it is inappropriate to promise that everyone on a waiting list will be treated within eighteen months. This could mean that some will wait longer than they should, whilst others not as long as they could reasonably be expected to. Consequently, serious drawbacks are likely to follow from undermining the traditional contribution of professional judgement in determining the type and quality of care to be offered.

Second, standards must be, to some extent, arbitrary. The aim, of course, is to raise everyone up to the standard of the best. However, current variations in standards cannot be explained simply in terms of variable efficiency. The wide range of factors which impinge upon the delivery of health care have to be considered and target standards set realistically. This will inevitably result in some levelling down as well as levelling up. Indeed, some commentators have suggested that targets are not ambitious enough. A spokesperson for the Patients' Association and the President of the Institute of Health Services Management agree that the government's standards merely list things that ought to be done in a well run service anyway (*Health Service Journal*, 7 November 1991).

Third, at whatever level the standard is set, the intention is that it is a minimum below which no one should fall. However, past experience suggests that this is not likely to work in practice. The history of social policy is littered with examples of minimum standards which become maximums, from the 'Allowance System' introduced in the parish of Speenhamland in the eighteenth century, where the intended minimum wage became, in practice, an income ceiling above which no worker could rise, to Beveridge's 'national minimum standard' in the 1940s which served to create the infamous poverty trap which has persistently characterized the British welfare state since.

Nevertheless, these points do not amount to a convincing argument against a Charter. Although not central, such things as waiting times are important, and guidelines for good practice, within which professional judgements are made, can be helpful. The much more powerful argument against a Charter is the fact that the pursuit of good practice in peripheral matters could well be at the expense of good practice in the central areas. Directing attention and resources to waiting lists, dissemination of information and so forth can divert valuable resources away from the more central issues affecting health and health care. 'The outcome for patients may well be undesirable if the focus of concern moves away from the comfort and care of the patient towards the achievement of crude, mechanistic targets such as waiting times' (Baggott, 1994, p. 197).

The danger that the priorities of the care givers will be distorted increases if pay and promotion are affected by performance with respect to standards. Professionals, very reasonably, will concentrate their efforts in the areas upon which they are judged. There is a very real danger that 'individuals and organizations . . . seek simply to achieve their targets rather than deliver a service' (*The Observer*, 2 July 1995). Indeed, where maximizing personal income and promotion prospects are given priority, patient care could well deteriorate.

The right to a maximum eighteen-month waiting time for hospital treatment has illustrated some of the distortion which can arise. The reduction in two-year waits from 50,000 in March 1991 to zero a year later was accompanied by an equally dramatic decline in the number of patients waiting between one and two years. However, the total number of patients waiting for treatment remained constant at around 900,000 because those waiting under one year (by far the largest group on the waiting list) had actually increased by 5 per cent.

This tendency helps to explain why many critics in the professional media fear that the Charter will result in 'hernias and hips' being given priority over more serious, urgent and complex treatments. The phrase 'pay-related performance' has an ominous ring to it in the context of health care, since it is quite possible to meet targets without achieving what was intended by setting them (*The Observer*, 2 July 1995).

At a much broader level, there is a further problem of distortion. One of the consequences of focusing on delivery is that the Charter necessarily concentrates narrowly on curative care. It is concerned to establish rights to treatment rather than rights to health. Whilst there is nothing wrong with this in itself, it endorses rather than challenges a traditional weakness of the NHS, that is, that it is a sickness rather than a health service, and runs counter to the current trend, advocated by the government itself, to concentrate efforts on staying healthy. Given what is now known about the social factors which contribute to health and illness, and the relatively minor role of formal health services, it is indisputable that the promotion and maintenance of health can be pursued only through strategies directed at society at large. The relationship between the Patient's Charter and citizenship is, therefore, highly relevant in this context.

The Patient's Charter and citizenship

The NHS is a striking example of a public service grounded in the notion of citizenship and the government was clearly intent upon placing charters in the context of citizenship. The Patient's Charter is one of the spin-off charters of the Citizen's Charter initiative and its emphasis on rights to health care is a pointed reminder of the founding values of the NHS. In 1948, just before the new NHS was launched, the Central Office of Information published a leaflet in which the public were told:

> Your new National Health Service begins on 5 July. It will provide you with all medical, dental and nursing care. Everyone – rich or poor, man, woman or child – can use it or part of it. There are no charges, except for a few special items. There are no insurance qualifications. But it is not a charity. You are all paying for it, mainly as taxpayers and it will relieve your money worries in times of illness.

From this statement it is clear that the NHS was intended to be comprehensive, universal, equally available to all, free at the point of use and financed out of taxation. Despite the many changes since the inception of the NHS, and the ideology of the government which has held power since 1979, these values have never been formally renounced. In 1979, the Merrison Commission listed seven similar principles and in the introduction to *Working For Patients* the government stated:

> The principles which have guided [the NHS] for the last forty years will continue to guide it into the twenty-first century. The NHS is, and will continue to be, open to all regardless of income, and financed mainly out of general taxation (Department of Health, 1989).

In similar vein, in October 1991, William Waldegrave, at the Conservative Party conference, reaffirmed his party's commitment to 'the fundamental unchanging principles of our health service, free and equal access to the very best in health care when you need it, regardless of means' (*The Guardian*, 11 October 1991).

In short, the NHS is not morally neutral, rather it represents very clearly a collectivist stance with respect to health and health care, recognizing both that the health of individuals impinges on the health status of the community at large and that individuals cannot look after all aspects of their own health. They may not have the financial means and knowledge to do so and rarely are they in a position to exercise full control over those aspects of their lives known to affect health, such as where they work and live, the air they breathe and the food they eat. It is, therefore, in the interests of the community at large to maintain the health of all its members because health carries 'external benefits' and consequently a measure of collectivism is necessary and is to be found in all developed polities (see, for example, Wall, 1996).

In short, the NHS has always been seen as public good which the state has a duty to provide and the population a right to use. At first sight the Charter emphasis on rights and declaration in the foreword that

> . . . there must be no change to the fundamental principles on which it [the NHS] was founded and on which it has continued ever since, namely that services should be available to every citizen on the basis of clinical need, regardless of ability to pay, and that the service should in the future, as in the past, mainly be paid for out of general taxation (Department of Health, 1991a, p. 4)

appears to endorse the founding values of the NHS and its contribution to the enhancement of citizenship. However, this is not the case. The Charter is unlikely to do anything to promote citizenship. The notion of citizenship is essentially collectivist in character, composed of the twin concepts of rights and obligations. The Patient's Charter is antithetical to this in that it individualizes members of society as consumers of health services. Some of the dilemmas, to which the dichotomy between consumer and citizen gives rise, are briefly discussed below.

Patients, as consumers, use the NHS but citizens, as tax payers, pay for it. Therefore, the NHS has a responsibility to the public at large, as well as to individual patients. Where the interests of these two constituencies clash, the Charter directs health care providers to give priority to individual patients. For example, achieving the eighteen-month target for surgery for a patient may not represent the best use of the public's resources.

Because health care confers benefits on society at large as well as on individuals, the individual patient cannot be the only consideration when health care decisions are made. Respecting the privacy and dignity of a patient with AIDS may jeopardize the health of the community at large.

The Charter also fails to recognize that many citizens do not achieve the status of patient. Only some citizens are patients. This is not simply because some are not in need, but is due to the fact that access to health services is unequal. Many of the poorest, least articulate members of society, and those marginalized through discrimination, are less likely to visit a GP, attend an out-patient clinic, or become an in-patient. In other words, there are targets relating to those on waiting lists but the barriers facing some citizens in their attempt to get onto a waiting list are overlooked. If the Charter does anything at all to promote citizenship it will be with respect primarily to the white middle class whose citizenship is already well established.

Furthermore, by focusing on rights to and standards in formal health care services, the emphasis of the Charter is necessarily on the public rather than private domain. This raises important gender issues. Women play a smaller part in the public world than men, but a larger part in the private world of promoting health within families and the informal care of the sick and dependent. Thus the citizenship of women is even less likely to be enhanced than that of men.

Evaluation of the Charter

For many involved in the delivery and use of health care services, these broad issues may appear very remote. For them the important questions are: how long a patient has to wait; whether patients have the information necessary to make a choice between hospitals; and whether one health authority is better than another with respect to meeting standards.

As a tool to judge the 'quality' of health care, therefore, the Charter may be useful. It offers yardsticks for the evaluation of performance; guidelines for service delivery and a mechanism for the dissemination of good practice. Its emphasis on giving patients information is particularly important since this is a major way of empowering people and lack of information and poor communication are two of the main complaints made by patients. Although many of the areas covered by the Charter could be said to be peripheral, this does not mean they are unimportant. Moreover, indicating to patients the targets in these areas, and providing them with more information about health services generally, may serve to raise their awareness and encourage them to start asking questions about more central issues.

In this sense, the Charter can be judged a genuine, if naive, attempt by a responsible government to improve health status by improving health services and confirming that access to good quality care is part of the rights of citizenship.

The arguments against such a conclusion centre around three issues:

- whether the Charter is likely to work in practice;
- if so, will it have the desired beneficial effects on the deficiencies of the NHS and the health status of the population; and
- whether it is likely to have any ill effects on health and health care.

With respect to the first of these, the improbability of resources being made available to rectify failure to achieve standards or maintain rights and devolving most of the responsibility for achieving the standards from the government will ultimately emasculate the Charter.

The second issue relates to the appropriateness of a Charter in the context of health. We already have rights to health care and the Charter adds little to these. Such rights can be couched only in the broadest of terms. They provide little in the way of protection or guarantees to patients. Standards are likely to be set fairly arbitrarily and to focus on measurable, peripheral aspects of health care.

Finally, arguably, in adopting a legalistic approach and focusing on measurable aspects of curative care and individual illness episodes, the Charter could distort the priorities of health care professionals, undermine the effectiveness of patient care, and divert attention and resources from the real issues of underfunding and prerequisites for health. In this regard, there is a danger that an important aspect of true citizenship will be denied to large numbers of people.

The alternative interpretation is that the Charter is a clever, devious political expedient to erode professional power and, since professionals have scant regard for the public purse, thereby effectively curb spending and, at the same time, throw a veil over fears about underfunding, privatization, and the erosion of the founding principles of the NHS.

References and further reading

Baggott, R. (1994), *Health and Health Care in Britain*, London, St. Martin's Press.
Barnsley Health Authority (1992), *Patient's Charter, Barnsley*, Barnsley Health Authority.
Bosanquet, N. (1982), 'Industrial Relations in the NHS after the Breakdown of the Old Colonial System', *Public Administration Bulletin*, no. 40.
Department of Health (1989), *Working for Patients*, HMSO, London.
Department of Health (1991a), *The Patient's Charter*, HMSO, London.
Department of Health (1991b), *The Health of the Nation: A Consultative Document for Health in England*, Cm 1523, HMSO, London.

Department of Health (1992), *The Health of the Nation: A Strategy for Health in England*, Cm 1986, HMSO, London.

Department of Health (1995), *The Patient's Charter and You*, HMSO, London.

Department of Health and Social Security (1980), *Inequalities in Health*, HMSO, London.

Dillner, L. (1991), Comment in *British Medical Journal*, vol. 303, 9 November, pp. 1153–54.

Hart, J. (1991), Comment in *British Medical Journal*, vol. 303, 9 November, p. 1158.

Marshall, T.H. (1963), 'Citizenship and Social Class', in T.H. Marshall, *Sociology at the Crossroads*, Heinemann, London.

National Health Service Management Executive (1992), *NHSME News*, no. 54, February.

O'Keefe, E., Ottewill, R. and Wall, A. (1992), *Community Health: Issues in Management*, Business Education Publishers Limited, Sunderland.

Royal Commission on the NHS (1979), *Report of the Royal Commission on the NHS* (Chairman Alexander W. Merrison), Cmnd 7615, HMSO, London.

Sheffield Health Authority (undated), *Sheffield's Patient's Charter*, Sheffield Health Authority, Sheffield.

Stocking, B. (1991), Comment in *British Medical Journal*, vol. 303, 9 November, p. 1148.

Taylor, D. (1991), 'A Big Idea for the Nineties? The Rise of the Citizens' Charters', *Critical Social* Policy, Issue 33, Winter 1991–92.

Wall, A. (ed.) (1996), *Health Care Systems in Liberal Democracies*, Routledge, London (in press).

Warden, J. (1991), Comment in *British Medical Journal*, vol. 303, 9 November, p. 1153.

8 The Charter and Education

ROBERT LEACH

The impact of Charters on education

Superficially education is at the centre of the application of Charter principles. The service featured prominently, coming second only to the NHS, in the original Citizen's Charter in July 1991 (Cabinet Office, 1991). The education section (pp. 13–14) described the purpose of recent government reforms in schools in terms of raising standards, promoting parental influence and choice, and securing better use of resources. 'The Citizen's Charter', it was claimed, 'reinforces these principles and carries them further'. Specifically the Charter promised independent inspection of schools, 'a parents' charter', information on the comparative performance of local education authorities from the Audit Commission, the publication by schools of exam results and levels of truancy, comparative information on schools, and an annual report for parents on each school child's progress. A year on, in the first report on the Citizen's Charter (Cabinet Office, 1992), the government could claim that much of this had been delivered. The new independent inspectorate, OFSTED, was in the process of being established, the Parent's Charters for England, Wales and Scotland had been issued, and most of the information promised had been or was soon to be published. In addition, it was announced that the Charter principles were to be extended to further and higher education, a pledge formally fulfilled with the publication of charters for both sectors by the Department for Education in 1993. The following year the momentum was apparently maintained by the issue of a new updated Parent's Charter (Department for Education, 1994). Moreover, as in the NHS, more specific institutional charters have been published, as individual colleges responded to John Patten's expectation that they should 'develop their own detailed charters within this national framework by summer 1994' (Department for Education, 1993a, p. 2), and some universities have produced their own documents.

All this activity would seem to indicate that the Citizen's Charter has had a major impact throughout the education service. Yet there are reasons for thinking that the implementation of the Charter principles has been particularly problematic for education.

In the first place, the Citizen's Charter and subsequent charters have initiated relatively little which was positively new in the field of education. Major changes had already been introduced in schools, culminating in the 1988 Education Reform Act. Thus the Citizen's Charter could only promise to 'reinforce' the principles behind the changes, and carry them further (Cabinet Office, 1991, p. 13). Similarly the Parent's Charter (Department for Education, 1994, p. 1) could only imply that the charters had 'played their part' in changes and in claimed improvements in standards and choice.

In further and higher education very important changes have been introduced under the Major government, including allowing the former polytechnics to become universities and removing further education from local authority control, but these had little to do with the Charter as such. Indeed, partly because of these upheavals, the application of Citizen's Charter principles to further and higher education was effectively delayed and until very recently has had less obvious impact (except possibly on the payment of mandatory grants), although it is now causing some ferment at institutional level. For this reason, this chapter will concentrate substantially on the application of the Charter to schools, where the impact came earlier, was more pronounced and better publicized.

Moreover, there were other reasons why the response to the Charter within education was underwhelming. Educational administrators, both in institutions and local government, had already taken on board a succession of initiatives concerned with customer care and service quality, including mission statements, performance review, the public service orientation, quality assurance and, in some areas, local citizen's charters (Sanderson, 1992). The Prime Minister's Citizen's Charter initiative extensively overlapped with all these developments and appeared to offer little that was really distinctive.

There were also more fundamental reasons why the implementation of Charter principles in education was always likely to be particularly problematic. The output of the service is particularly complex and notoriously difficult to measure. There are fundamental differences over the very nature and purpose of education, as well as technical problems in measuring performance. There are some difficulties of control in that the Department for Education and Employment has to rely in part on local education authorities (LEAs) as intermediaries in the administration of the Charter. A more significant obstacle is perhaps that the education service is, at the point of delivery, effectively under the control of professionals who have their own professional values and standards, and tend to be resistant to standards imposed from outside. Moreover, there are some inherent problems in invoking consumer sovereignty as a counterweight to professional dominance, as in schools the Charter has to rely on parents as proxies for the real consumers of education services.

Finally, there is some empirical evidence that the Citizen's Charter and the Parent's Charter have not had a significant impact on teachers, educational administrators or parents. Beale and Pollitt (1994) discovered from surveys in schools that some teaching and administrative staff had not even heard of or seen a copy of the Parent's Charter, and in general there was little knowledge of the principles or requirements of the Charter. Particularly in comparison with other services, such as out-patients' units in hospitals, it appeared that 'the Charters had little impact on the education service, except in terms of customer complaints about the allocation of places'.

This conclusion has to be set against the market research conducted by the Central Office of Information (November 1994) on the response to the updated Parent's Charter, distributed to 20 million homes in England, which found that 58 per cent of a representative sample had heard of the Charter, some eight weeks after distribution, although strikingly only 29 per cent claimed to recognize the booklet when shown a copy.

Some commentators have suggested that the whole Citizen's Charter initiative indicates a significant change in the government's attitude towards the public services, reflecting a marked difference in the underlying philosophy of John Major compared with his predecessor, Margaret Thatcher (Riddell, 1994; Kavanagh, 1994; Willman, 1994). Yet it was soon also clear that this commitment to public services for Major's government was quite compatible with the energetic pursuit of privatization, market testing and competition. It may thus be questioned whether the Charter was part of an essentially new agenda, or a novel means of promoting the old agenda.

There is a similar question mark over the attitude of the Major government more specifically towards education. Thus Scott (1994, p. 343) argues:

> The Prime Minister's preoccupation with improving public services through the Citizen's Charter, and the origins of both Mr Clarke and Mr Patten on the 'left' of the party have increased the emphasis on improving state schools at the expense of aiding the independent sector.

Others would suggest that this apparent commitment to state education has concentrated on a small proportion of the state sector, arguably with some adverse consequences for the remainder, and has not been reflected in increased resources for the educational service generally. The higher standards proclaimed in the charters are to be achieved by improved efficiency, with no extra money, and indeed a continuing squeeze on resources.

Ostensibly the Citizen's Charter involves the application of some relatively uncontroversial principles for the administration of public services like education. Much of the language of the charters appears clear, straightforward and relatively uncontentious. Rights are being publicized, standards established, targets set, information provided, performance measured, all with the aim of improving choice, quality and achieving better value for money. If analysis of the impact of the charters begins with the documents themselves and proceeds to their implementation in various services such as education, there is a tendency to accept too uncritically proclaimed intentions. It is important to look at the charters, not in relative isolation, but in the context of general government policy, and more specifically here, education policy.

The New Right and Conservative education policy

The ideas sometimes characterized under the label 'Thatcherism' or the 'New Right', are perhaps best understood as a blend of neoliberal free market ideas coupled with more traditional conservative themes. Education has been subject to both an extensive neoliberal and a neoconservative critique, with far-reaching policy implications.

The neoliberal critique suggested that state education suffered from the same absence of competition as other state services. In the absence of market pressures it was run by public service professionals in their own interests without regard for the real wishes of consumers. New Right think tanks such as the Institute of Economic Affairs proposed education vouchers as a means of effectively empowering consumers, but although this idea has been regularly canvassed, successive Conservative governments shied away from such a revolutionary proposal in favour of injecting competition and market choice into the service by other means. Thus the government has pursued administrative decentralization and extensive budgetary delegation, in accordance with the recommendations of public choice theorists.

The neoliberal critique has been paralleled by a another approach which might be dubbed 'neoconservative', except that it had earlier found some expression in the Great Education Debate launched by the Labour Premier Callaghan in the wake of the publication of education 'Black Papers'. This critique attacked the dominance of a trendy progressive educational elite, perceived as responsible for a decline in traditional standards, values and discipline. Concern was expressed over the content of the curriculum (e.g. the neglect of the classics in English literature, neglect of British history), over methods (individual and group work rather than whole class work, projects rather than exams) and over standards (especially in maths, spelling and grammar). Some also hankered after a return to selection and the old grammar school ethos.

These two critiques were at bottom inspired by different philosophies. The classical liberal assumption is of course that individuals are the best judges of their own interests, while the conservative emphasis on authority and discipline involved some paternalist assumptions plainly at variance with the liberal doctrine. Even so, much of their analysis and prescription was compatible. Both, for different reasons, were hostile to professional dominance, and both sought to empower parents as a counterweight to teachers. However, a clear potential for conflict existed where consumer sovereignty and market choice did not necessarily coincide with cherished values. What if the customers did not want Shakespeare, or religious education, or team games?

Besides these ideological considerations there were more pragmatic electoral concerns over education, widely seen as an important issue for voters, and especially for the Conservatives' own middle-class constituency, some of whom were torn between the prohibitive cost of private schooling and the perceived horrors of the neighbourhood comprehensive.

Both the Thatcher and Major governments have sought to meet these concerns, and in so doing have implemented elements of both the neoliberal and neoconservative agendas. Various education policies can be seen in terms of advancing the neoliberal free market agenda. The assisted places scheme, involving subsidies for those who wanted private education for their children but could not afford it, could be justified in terms of enlarging competition and choice. Over time the government offered other 'exit options' for those dissatisfied with ordinary LEA schools, including city technology colleges and, more particularly, grant-maintained schools. More important in the immediate term was the establishment of a quasi-market or internal market, through the Local Management of Schools initiative, coupled with a funding formula based on pupil numbers and open enrolment, under which schools were effectively compelled to compete for pupils. A statutory obligation on schools to provide increasing quantities of information, particularly on exam results, assisted parental choice.

Yet other educational reforms were not particularly inspired by a free market philosophy. The national curriculum and the associated national tests may make comparisons between schools easier, and thus assist consumer choice, but they involve a standardization of content and to some extent method which has little to do with the classical liberal emphasis on freedom and choice.

Moreover John Major's premiership has not involved any marked shift in approach from this blend of neoliberalism and traditional conservatism, certainly towards school education. The changes embodied in the Education Reform Act of 1988 have been energetically pursued. Local management of schools has been extensively implemented. If anything, the Major government has been more enthusiastic about encouraging schools to opt out of LEA control. Although obliged to make some concessions to the teaching profession over administration of testing, the government has finally forced through its tests on the national curriculum. Moreover, John Major's ill-starred 'back to basics' campaign reflected traditional conservative concerns over moral standards and discipline. John Patten, as Secretary of State for Education, placed particular emphasis on religious education, and attempted to enforce statutory obligations on the curriculum and daily acts of worship which have been widely ignored.

The Parent's Charter in context

Seen against this background, the Parent's Charter does not signal some new concern with state education, but is thoroughly consistent with past policies. Indeed the role of the Parent's Charter was essentially to publicize those policies and further assist their implementation. Thus the Charter begins: 'Schools have changed a lot in recent years. Standards have improved, and there is wider choice . . . This updated Parent's Charter tells you all about these improvements.'

The wider choice is subsequently explained partly in terms of 'types of school' in a section where 'self-governing schools', city technology colleges and the assisted places scheme are all advertised. It is stated that 'the Government expects the number of self-governing schools to increase greatly over the next few years'. Here the Charter is effectively promoting government policy.

The Citizen's Charter is of course to do with citizens' rights, and among the rights proclaimed in the Parent's Charter is a 'right to a school place for your child from age 5 to age 16' coupled with a 'right to a place in the school you want unless all the places at the school have been given to pupils who have a stronger claim to a place at that school' (pp. 9–10). The Charter goes on to point out that schools have to explain their admission policy in their prospectus, and cannot normally keep places empty, but effectively concedes the practical constraints on parental choice. 'A school which does not have room for the pupils who have applied for places cannot expand automatically to provide more room.' However, the Charter suggests that 'more places can be put into popular schools' as 'spare places in less popular schools are taken out of use' (Department for Education, 1994, p. 13). The mechanics by which this transfer of places is to take place is not explained, nor is there any mention of the resources available to fund it. Procedures for appealing against the refusal of a place are, however, subsequently explained in some detail.

The right to information is another key aspect of the Citizen's Charter, and this too is outlined in the Parent's Charter. Thus parents have a right to a report about the progress of their child, a right of information about reports on schools by inspectors, a right to a free copy of performance tables for local schools on exams, truancy and other matters, the right to a school prospectus, a right to a copy of the annual school governors' report, coupled with a right to attend the associated annual parents' meeting. In substance, some of this is hardly new, and only follows common practice, but clearer and more stringent requirements are laid down.

Much of this can be welcomed in terms of open government and publicizing rights. Yet some of it at least is closely tied in with development of competition and choice, and an effective 'internal market' within education. Parents are promised more choice and the information necessary to make that choice. The corollary is that schools are effectively competing for pupils. Indeed competition is at the heart of the government's approach towards public services, as summed up succinctly in the 1991 White Paper *Competing for Quality*, published under the auspices of the Citizen's Charter. 'Competition is the best guarantee of quality and value for money' (Treasury, 1991, p. 1). This is also the approach that underlies the Parent's Charter, even if there is little explicit reference there to the values of competition.

This is why exam league tables have caused so much angst among teachers. Apparently poor results could lead to fewer new pupils and a downward spiral towards ultimate closure unless the school performance is perceived to improve. Indeed this is how the system is supposed to work, rewarding success, penalizing failure, and promoting higher standards through competition. Yet many teachers protest that this information does not give a fair picture of the school's efficiency and achievements, as it does not allow for the considerable differences in the background and prior educational achievements of pupils. To an extent the Department for Education has attempted to respond to these concerns, and has explored ways of measuring 'value added' in education, but it is not yet clear whether this will lead to a national system for reporting and publishing reliable indicators (Department for Education, 1995).

More sophisticated statistical information is likely to present particular difficulties for presentation and interpretation. Indeed some would object that such statistics, however refined and sophisticated, can never present an accurate picture of a school's real achievement and output. In concentrating on the more easily quantifiable aspects of the education process, such as exam results or truancy tables, there is a danger that other important but less tangible educational objectives, such as personal development and social integration, may be undervalued. Behind this debate over the presentation of information lie some continuing unresolved differences over the whole purpose of education.

The Audit Commission and performance indicators

Exam league tables are only one form of performance indicators that have been introduced into the education service. Also under the auspices of the Citizen's Charter, the Audit Commission is now required by law (Local Government Act 1992) to draw up a set of indicators for measuring the performance of local authority services, including education, 'to inform the public about the standards of performance of their council and to facilitate comparisons with other councils and from one year to another' (Audit Commission, 1991, p. 1)

Following consultation, the Audit Commission issued its first list of performance indicators on which information was required at the end of 1992, for the financial year 1993/94, which Councils had to publish locally between April and December 1994. The Audit Commission proceeded to publish summary details of comparative performance in 1995. On education the Audit Commission published information on LEA performance, with some caveats, on the provision of school places for the under-fives, on expenditure per pupil for primary and secondary pupils, on the assessment of children with special needs, and on the payment of mandatory student grants (Audit Commission, 1995, pp. 7–23).

Although the Audit Commission has proceeded cautiously and as far as possible on the basis of consultation and consensus, and has been suitably careful in interpreting the results, the education performance indicators only serve to illustrate the limitations of such statistics. One of the main indicators, on expenditure per pupil, is only a measure of input, not of output, and certainly not of outcome. As the Audit Commission makes clear at the outset in a general caveat, 'you should not assume that a higher figure is always better than a lower one' (p. 8). Higher spending may indicate a better service, or less efficiency. The big differences in the ratio between spending on primary and secondary pupils to which the Audit Commission draws attention is certainly interesting, but as the Commission indicates:

> There is no clear cut answer to the question of what should be the proper balance of funding between secondary and primary pupils and the best the performance indicators can do is help inform the debate (1995, p. 11).

Comparative statistics on the speed of completion of assessment and statements for pupils with special needs and of the payments of mandatory student grants are more truly performance indicators. Moreover they do reveal some significant differences in performance, particularly on special needs (where indeed the Department for Education has taken some trouble to outline rights and procedures, both in the updated Parent's Charter and in supplementary public documents). Yet important though these indicators of performance are to those directly concerned, they necessarily emphasize aspects of the service that are more easily quantified. Like performance indicators for other services (e.g. waiting lists for hospital treatment) they tell us little about the real quality of the service. It is always likely that measurement will by itself have a tonic effect, but perhaps at the expense of the neglect of some other parts of the service which are not subject to measurement.

The most interesting comparative statistics are those on the provision of school places for the under-fives, with very wide differences between councils on this discretionary aspect of educational provision. Yet these bald statistics are only very imperfect measures of performance. As the Audit Commission points out, 'providing school places is not the only way in which councils help the under-fives.' Moreover, it is not even clear how far the differences in provision are the consequence of conscious decision. As with comparative figures on spending per pupil, the most such statistics can do is help to inform the debate.

In fact, similar comparative statistics have previously been published annually by other bodies, such as the Chartered Institute for Public Finance and Accountancy. The Audit Commission's work has the authoritative sanction of the law behind it, and perhaps as a consequence the figures are more reliable, and will secure wider publicity. Yet although the prime criterion for selection of indicators is 'interest to citizens' it is not always clear what use the citizen can make of the information provided. With some performance indicators published under the auspices of the Citizen's Charter it is possible to measure performance against published standards, and seek redress if the published standards are not met (for example, punctuality of trains). Yet it is by no means obvious what a parent seeking a school place for an under-five is to make of the information provided about local council provision. There is no clear standard or right to a place, and they can only have recourse to the usual political remedies of lobbying and the ballot.

This highlights the point that such widely publicized information can, and perhaps should, be used for political purposes. This does, however, raise in acute form the criteria for selecting performance indicators by public bodies at all levels. If the performance of local authorities can be judged in part by the resources they make available for primary and secondary education, and on the places they provide for the under-fives, on a comparative basis with other councils, it might equally be urged that comparative statistics should be similarly published on the resources western governments devote to education and on various other indicators, such as class sizes.

Empowering parents

Applying the principles of the Citizen's Charter to education would seem to be in large part about empowering parents. The very title 'Parent's Charter' is significant. It might have been called a charter for school pupils or more neutrally a charter for schools. To be fair, the title of the updated Parent's Charter is 'Our Children's Education' and it is clear from some of the content that the possessive adjective is meant to encompass the whole community and not just parents, and indeed it was circulated to all households. Even so, the main thrust is about the rights of parents, and reflects a clear agenda of shifting power from the professional providers of education to parents.

For neoliberals what this is all about is consumer sovereignty, with parents as surrogates for the real service users, the children. There are of course some problems here. As Beale and Pollitt (1994) observe, stating the obvious, parents are 'seldom present at the point of service delivery'. All the information with which parents are now regaled is scarcely a substitute for direct experience of the service. Most of the knowledge they pick up is through the dubiously reliable source of their own offspring. Moreover, the classical liberal assumption about individuals rationally pursuing their own interests can scarcely be automatically extended to their children's interest. The child's interest might conflict with the parent's interest – a school might be chosen on the grounds of parental convenience or presumed social cachet rather than the child's own need or preference. Even if it can be assumed that parents have the interests of their child at heart, they may not be the best judge of that interest.

In some respects the role accorded to parents in education goes rather beyond New Right radical consumerism, with an emphasis on a representative role in school decision-making, through the election of parent governors, and a crucial right to determine, through a postal ballot, whether their childrens' school should opt out of local authority control. These rights, contained in earlier legislation, are explicitly acknowledged and publicized in the Parent's Charter.

For traditional conservatives, giving a larger role to parents has more to do with family and other values. Parents should be obeyed. They have rights, but also obligations, which they should be encouraged or obliged to undertake. This too is a strand of thinking that is explicitly recognized in the Parent's Charter. Moreover, those critical of what they see as the trendy progressiveness of the professional educational establishment see parents as allies in pursuit of traditional discipline, content and method. One parental right explicitly recognized in the Charter is the right to withdraw children from lessons involving sex education, a right reflecting the view of some conservatives that sex education is a matter for parents rather than schools. The right of withdrawal coupled with an explicit requirement that the governors' policy on sex education must be published in the school prospectus arguably places some constraints on the dissemination of knowledge. Here, deference to parental authority might be held to conflict with the longer-term interests of the child and perhaps of society.

In some respects empowering parents has not worked out quite as some radicals of the right have anticipated. Most notably, the rapid growth of grant-maintained schools has not proceeded as the government envisaged, with parental ballots producing a heavy preponderance against opting out, often against the recommendations of governors, and despite the offer of considerable financial inducements. Moreover, parents by and large have not presented a counterweight to the vested interests of public service professionals. Rather they have tended to side with teachers on a range of issues, including testing and the crucial question of educational resources.

Both the Citizen's Charter as a whole and the education charters reflect a government conviction that it is possible to make radical improvements in service quality by achieving better value for money without additional resources. It does seem likely that some efficiency savings have indeed been achieved through delegated budgets, which has provided an incentive for energy saving measures in schools and promoted a hard reappraisal of the nature and extent of some services supplied to schools (e.g. ground maintenance). Thus there has been some reallocation of priorities and spending within budgets which has been generally beneficial. But most of these savings have been at the margin, and are of a once and for all nature. The bulk of schools' budgets consists of the salaries of teaching staff, and further significant savings can only be made here. Those who think quality in education may have something to do with class sizes argue that additional resources are necessary. This goes to the heart of the assumptions behind the Charter initiative.

References and further reading

Audit Commission (1991), *The Citizen's Charter: Local Authority Performance Indicators*, HMSO, London.

Audit Commission (1992), *Citizen's Charter Performance Indicators*, HMSO, London.

Audit Commission (1993), *Staying on Course: The Second Year of the Citizen's Charter Indicators*, HMSO, London.

Audit Commission (1994), *Watching Their Figures: A Guide to the Citizen's Charter Indicators*, HMSO, London.

Audit Commission (1995), *Local Authority Performance Indicators*, vol 1, HMSO, London.

Beale, V. and Pollitt, C. (1994), 'Charters at the Grass Roots: a First Report', *Local Government Studies*, vol. 20, no. 2.

Cabinet Office (1991), *The Citizen's Charter*, Cm 1599, HMSO, London.

Cabinet Office (1992), *The Citizen's Charter, First Report: 1992*, Cm 2101, HMSO, London.

Central Office of Information Research (1994), *Summary of Findings: Parents Charter Research*, Central Office of Information, London.

Department for Education (1993a), *The Charter for Further Education*, HMSO, London.

Department for Education (1993b), *The Charter for Higher Education*, HMSO, London.

Department for Education (1994), *Our Children's Education: The Updated Parent's Charter*, HMSO, London.

Department for Education (1995), *Value Added in Education: A Briefing Paper from the Department for Education*, HMSO, London.

Kavanagh, D. (1994), 'A Major Agenda?' in Kavanagh, D. and Seldon, A. (eds), *The Major Effect*, Macmillan, London.

Riddell, P. (1994), 'Ideology in Practice', in Adonis, A. and Hames, T. (eds), *A Conservative Revolution? The Thatcher-Reagan Decade in Perspective*, Manchester University Press, Manchester.

Sanderson, Ian (ed.) (1992), *Management of Quality in Local Government*, Longman, Harlow.

Scott, P. (1994), 'The Civil Service', in Kavanagh, D. and Seldon, A. (eds), *The Major Effect*, Macmillan, London.

Treasury (1991), *Competing for Quality*, Cm 1730, HMSO, London.

Willman, J. (1994), 'The Civil Service', in Kavanagh, D. and Seldon, A. (eds), *The Major Effect*, Macmillan, London.

9 The Citizen's Charter and Housing

BRIAN D. JACOBS

This chapter is concerned with the Citizen's Charter and housing. The focus is upon the implications of the Citizen's Charter mainly for housing in urban areas where there are high levels of social and economic distress. The Charter's main emphasis was upon the development of new non-local authority management arrangements and the transfer of public housing to the private sector. The Charter had important implications for the provision of housing in areas where there had traditionally been a high proportion of public social housing. There was therefore a clear link between the Charter's strategy for housing and the Conservative government's urban policy where privatization and enterprise remained key themes flowing from the Thatcher era.

This chapter critically appraises the Charter's housing provisions. The focus is upon the ideological underpinnings of its view of housing and the implications of associated policy prescriptions. The chapter is thus concerned with the role of housing in the Conservative government's broader urban policy. Mention is made of the attempts by the Major and Thatcher governments to privatize urban housing and move towards greater use of private sector involvement. In this way, housing played a key role both in the economic strategy to regenerate the 'inner cities' and in promoting the Thatcher dream of the 'enterprise culture'.

Partnerships involving the public and private sectors were encouraged by the Conservatives as mechanisms conducive to economic revival. Privatization and private investment were presented as part of an innovative urban policy strategy designed to encourage community self-help. This was linked to the involvement of companies and financial institutions in urban initiatives. There was also a desire to introduce private sector involvement into local services (including architecture and planning) by way of compulsory competitive tendering (Slavid, 1994). The hoped-for political spin-off, as far as the Conservatives were concerned, involved the gradual growth of a new privatized culture in urban communities which had traditionally been host to collectivist solutions to social housing and public service provision.

Prime Minister Thatcher believed that she could win the inner cities for the Conservatives. A key element in her political game plan was to privatize housing, partly by encouraging individual home ownership. John Major's Citizen's Charter reinforced this objective by seeking to define a reinvigorated agenda for run-down urban communities where large numbers of residents lived in local authority-owned housing.

The Citizen's Charter codified much of what the Conservatives had to say on housing in the 1980s and early 1990s. Its concern with housing was more than just a public relations statement of vague policy commitments. It provided a sharper policy focus for politicians and government officials. It strengthened the government's strategic political purpose as part of a proactive approach to achieving the objectives of privatization and community 'empowerment'. This was done by involving communities in housing management, extending home ownership and increasing the role of private sector financing in housing.

The ideological underpinnings

The policy context was one in which housing and urban decline became an important policy concern of the Conservative New Right during the 1980s. Charles Murray (1984), who became popular amongst British Conservatives and prominent Cabinet members, identified an 'underclass' in the inner cities. The underclass consisted of people who were dependent upon the state for welfare provisions. For Murray, governments traditionally regarded public expenditure on welfare support as one means of overcoming the immediate problems created by economic decline, unemployment and poverty. However, this welfare support created an inertia whereby the underclass existed in a state of dependency upon the state. The solution for Murray and the New Right lay with the removal of the 'big government' from the inner cities and the abandonment of a distinct 'urban policy' (Jacobs, 1993).

Murray described Britain as creating an American-style underclass. Significantly, he could come to this conclusion ten years after the election of Margaret Thatcher as prime minister. Her period of office had not affected the underlying processes producing greater welfare dependency. For Murray (1990, p. 2), the United States has 'reached the future first'.

Communities were developing a profound sense of demoralization. Crime, illegitimacy, homelessness and unemployment had all worsened in spite of the initiatives taken by government to overcome such problems. The underclass was growing and creating a situation where the unemployed had no experience of work. Communities were losing their will to help themselves.

Murray argued that the root causes of this situation had not been tackled. Welfare benefits continued at levels that provided a disincentive to the unemployed to find work. The social security system reflected a whole culture of dependency that produced low expectations within communities and blunted their potential for self-improvement and enterprise. The welfare benefits system was producing a major crisis exacerbating problems such as those arising from poor public housing. The welfare state was hampering the renewal of distressed communities. The collectivist notion that public expenditure could assist social and economic improvement was a fallacy. Tax-funded intervention strengthened the welfare-dependent culture and consolidated the economic decline of communities by stifling enterprise and innovation.

Murray called for 'a massive dose of self-government' where communities would learn to take initiatives for themselves. They would generate resources for improvements locally from the private sector. Communities would take control of the local decision-making process including the criminal justice system, education and housing. In short, Murray had taken up the American New Right's clarion call for community control and empowerment through self-help and local activism. It was a call that, in many respects, echoed the desires of 1960s welfare liberals for community control, but without public intervention to achieve it.

The new urban policy

There was little that was new in this approach. The Conservative Party was concerned about the problems of welfare dependency in the 1970s. Under the government of Edward Heath (1970–74), Sir Keith Joseph initiated research into the 'cycle of transmitted deprivation'. This research was conducted at the Department of Health and Social Security under Joseph's direction. It drew upon American experience where Conservatives had suggested a link between welfare dependency and the growth of crime and a breakdown in traditional social institutions such as the family. These were the opening shots of the right's concern with the family and church as providing the foundation for stable urban communities.

They were themes that were to be heard again in Britain following the Conservative's 1979 general election victory. They were also to emerge in the 1990s as the Major government's desire to get 'back to basics' and to strengthen traditional 'family values'. More importantly, the political agenda in urban policy shifted rightwards to accommodate the discussion of welfare dependency as a causal factor in the decline of distressed urban communities. It signified the 'roll back' of public intervention in urban policy and social housing. The collectivist 'solution' of public intervention was redefined by Conservatives as itself being 'the problem'. Collectivism no longer was a liberator of community energies; rather it was seen as an agent promoting disempowerment and public disillusion in planning, education and health.

This was graphically illustrated in urban policy in the 1980s, when there were a variety of influences upon Conservative thinking emanating from the New Right's thinking. While British Conservatives did not simply translate New Right prescriptions into practical policy, there was a change in the political agenda and in the public mood that made it easier for Conservatives to move against welfarism.

However the 'new urban policy' in Britain in the 1980s reflected contradictory policy objectives (Jacobs, 1993). In urban policy, the Conservatives combined privatism with a continued commitment to the centralized public funding of the Department of the Environment (DoE). The Government's Urban Programme, the City Challenge initiative and the newly created state-funded urban development corporations all represented continued state intervention in the market. In 1993, an integrated Urban Regeneration Budget was announced which was to rationalize the distribution of urban funds under one coordinated budget heading and further strengthen the role of the DoE.

Conservative themes

The Citizen's Charter was devised against this background of a partial assimilation of right-wing ideology within a centralized urban policy framework. By looking at some of the New Right's policy prescriptions on urban issues it is possible to discern some of the popular Conservative themes that are found in the Citizen's Charter which were applied to housing. The elements of this new urban agenda (indicated below) were often awkwardly drafted by the Thatcher government onto a large pre-existing governmental bureaucracy. As in the case of the government-supported Housing Corporation (which part-funded the expanding housing associations), there was actually an expansion in quasi-government as older forms of public intervention were replaced.

The prescriptions here should be taken as indicative of the ideas that were influential in placing commonly expressed Conservative themes onto the political agenda in the period since 1980. They should not necessarily be seen as specific to the Citizen's Charter, but more as being representative of the Conservative ideology characteristic of the period.

- There was the desire by American 'neo-liberals' (those Conservatives supportive of free market solutions and a reduced state) to abandon collectivist solutions to the problems of the cities. This was consistent with the view adopted by Charles Murray. The neo-liberal onslaught against public intervention had a history pre-dating the Murray analysis (Podhoretz, 1979).
- There was a strong economic case put forward by the right to support the contention that the state only makes matters worse. The Friedmans (1980) pointed to the benefits that the free market could bring communities. They saw government urban housing programmes as the cause of longer-term social problems and, like Murray, as placing a constraint on the development of local enterprise.
- In housing, the New Right favoured private initiative as a means of facilitating the 'empowerment' of tenants. In the 1980s, this was linked to the stimulation of economic activity in rundown communities.
- There was also the encouragement of non-profit organizations. Local economic development would provide communities with the capacity to do things for themselves and generate resources for change from within the community. In Britain, this kind of thinking was evident in the urban villages movement which had the support of influential private companies and organizations such as Business in the Community (BITC). It was BITC, with Prince Charles as its president, that was to the fore in fostering public/private sector partnerships in housing as part of the urban renewal process. It stressed the importance of the role of the voluntary sector and community involvement in planning and design.
- Another important strand coming from New Right thinking was that citizens should have responsibility for their own futures. This went

together with community 'empowerment'. Empowerment could be effective if communities recognized that they had certain social obligations. Following Lawrence Mead (1986), the New Right in the United States increasingly stressed the social obligation of citizens to work for welfare benefits. However, social obligation also referred to the development of skills of citizenship. People should be aware of their rights and also their obligations. Government had obligations to taxpayers and the communities that received tax-funded benefits. Here, there was a 'cosy' notion that both citizens and governments should operate within certain limits and that people were obligated to perform their social role in helping to keep government in line.

- Public choice theory was also influential (Lovrich and Neiman, 1984). Public choice theory provided the New Right with a theoretical foundation for defining community needs. It stressed the adverse effects of public bureaucracy on the overall welfare of society. Government itself and the bureaucrats in government, as allocators of resources, were at the heart of the problem. Government bureaucrats had a vested interest in perpetuating public intervention. They tended to expand budgets and provide subsidies and programmes that strengthened the welfare-dependent culture. Politicians accepted this provided that their constituencies benefited from the public funds that government provided. The result was that the market linkage between consumer needs and the provision of goods and services was distorted by the intervention of government and the vested interests of public officials.

Failed utopias

Apart from these ideological themes, the Conservatives' desire to move away from state provision was influenced by the poor record of public housing. The housing and building boom of the 1960s was accompanied by the popularity among local authorities of high-rise flats. These were often 'system built' and provided in the form of drab and regimented estates lacking the social cohesion of the 'slums' that they replaced. The utopian vision of the modernist architects was, however, short-lived. The disastrous effects of the high-rise blocks on community life were soon recognized.

Alice Coleman (1985), in *Utopia on Trial*, pointed to the poor condition of the housing estates created by the utopian vision of the future. Public social housing had been a failure since it destroyed personal identities and denied the value of private space. Coleman argued that collectivist solutions to housing problems had created more problems than they had solved (this being in line with the New Right view). Her call was for an end to the construction of the high-rise estates and an onslaught against the so-called 'housing bureaucracy' which she said resided in Britain's town halls. Coleman linked the problems of the estates to their design, layout and lack of community ownership. Her message was one that received the enthusiastic support of the Thatcher government. In 1988, Coleman was appointed by the DoE as a consultant to the Design Improvement Controlled Experiment (DICE) which involved the redesign of seven selected housing estates by involving tenants and local authorities.

The Council Tenant's Charter

These developments and the popularization in government of the views of the New Right help to contextualize the Citizen's Charter approach to housing. The Citizen's Charter, and the related Council Tenant's Charter, provided general guidelines for what the government intended to do about four main aspects of housing provision.

First, there was to be a clearer conception of rights and obligations concerning local authority tenants. Secondly, there would be increased opportunities for tenants to transfer housing estates away from local authority control and purchase their homes. They would be given more powers of control over their estates (a form of empowerment in the face of town hall bureaucracy). Thirdly, there was to be a stronger Tenant's Guarantee which would cover the rights of those living in housing association-owned properties. Finally, compulsory competitive tendering would be extended into the field of housing management, giving the private sector a greater role.

The Citizen's Charter and the Council Tenant's Charter combined both practical guidelines to be adhered to by local authorities with a controversial approach to housing management. In this respect, they provided a bittersweet menu for local authorities, especially those committed to public social housing. On the one hand, there were the aspects of the Charter that stressed tenants' rights and local authority obligations to tenants. These were intended to provide better information and services to tenants. The Council Tenant's Charter described the services local authorities should provide for tenants and indicated how tenants could become more involved in the management of estates. There was also guidance as to how the statutory rights of tenants could be practically implemented. On the other hand, the Council Tenant's Charter provided a statement of intent by the government about moving council estates further out of public control.

The Council Tenant's Charter covered the rights of tenants before the allocation of a council home. Tenants were alerted to the need of councils to publish short versions of their rules for deciding who gets homes. Applicants should have access to those rules. Where an applicant applied to a housing association, there were similar rights set out in 'The Tenant's Guarantee'.

The Council Tenant's Charter promoted the idea of local authority housing as a service that should be responsive to the customer. Council officials should, according to the Charter, 'be polite and helpful'. Public officials should wear name badges, have telephone answering machines and take messages when nobody is in the office (DoE, 1992, p. 8). So-called 'good councils' should ensure that applications are handled in confidence and that there is no discrimination against ethnic minority groups. Local authorities were encouraged to abide by the Code of Practice in Rented Housing produced by the Commission for Racial Equality, which called for non-discrimination and special provisions for ethnic minority applicants.

The Council Tenant's Charter pointed to important rights relating to security of tenure. Most people who rent from local authorities are 'secure tenants'. In essence, this concern of the Charter was about the need for councils to publish the details of tenancy agreements with a full description of the rights and obligations on both sides of any agreement. Councils were obliged to keep tenants informed and up to date concerning matters affecting tenancy agreements. They should explain in non-technical language what the agreements stipulate.

More controversially, the Council Tenant's Charter dealt with the tenant's right to buy. If they had been secure tenants for two years, house-holders enjoyed the right to buy their homes. The purchase of a home should be 'simple and straightforward', and there were rights to ensure that councils would process applications for purchase in a satisfactory manner.

The Council Tenant's Charter implied a general obligation concerning tenant awareness and involvement. There was a sense in which the Charter thus attempted to mobilize tenants actively to pursue goals that were regarded as being in their best interests. More precisely, tenants were encouraged to help themselves. This could be achieved by:

- tenants establishing just how their councils involve tenants in local authority initiatives;
- tenants insisting that they are properly consulted;
- individuals joining a tenant's group and making sure that the local authority consults the group in all plans;
- encouraging wide participation on estates and promoting interest in plans;
- replying to council questionnaires about what tenants want;
- giving the council ideas for improving estates and not just waiting for local authorities to do something;
- taking advantage of any training designed to enhance the role of tenants in running estates (DoE, 1992, p. 27).

The Council Tenant's Charter portrayed these activities as helping both the local authority and other tenants. Participation was a virtue that stimulated interest in local affairs and developed the management skills necessary for the efficient running of estates.

Taken together, these obligations provided an agenda for community activism. However, this was prescribed within limited bounds. It was orientated to the pursuance of the Charter's undisguised aim of privatizing local authority housing. Indeed, the stated 'right' to buy or 'right' to choose another landlord was effectively redefined when it became linked to the activist element. Rights became social 'obligations' once tenants were said to have a responsibility to be active and interested in the running of estates. In this role, tenants were cast as facilitators in the government's privatization strategy for social housing. This was something that was perfectly consistent with the New Right's conception of social obligations. It provided a strong basis for the undermining of state or municipal initiative in the provision of social housing.

Such an approach eclipsed the notion of a non-bureaucratic collectivist policy as an alternative model to that of privatized housing and community empowerment. The superficially similar idea of tenant's activism contained in socialist writing (Gould, 1988) in reality represented a very different future to that contained in the Citizen's Charter. A non-bureaucratic and publicly funded solution to the problems of council housing estates could conceivably be based upon diverse forms of cooperative and municipal ownership of housing estates.

Arrangements could allow for coordinated planning of estate facilities and services and could involve tenants in management decisions. There would not necessarily be an assumption of private ownership of estates, so properties in the public sector would not have to be exchanged within the market.

The Council Tenant's Charter advocated a different outcome: a market-led policy. Social housing was to be part of the mainstream private housing market. Housing associations and other landlords would be able to buy and sell properties and regulate the allocation of properties to applicants and existing tenants. As with houses, flats eventually entered the private market and their prices and rents were changed according to the longer-term trends and shortages evident in the market.

Large-scale voluntary housing transfers

How did the policy of marketization for the large council estates work in practice? This can be answered by reference to the privatization of public rented housing. One way of introducing the market and tenant management into housing was by way of large-scale voluntary transfers (LSVTs). This involved the voluntary transfer by local authorities of their housing stock to the private sector. By the end of 1993, 23 authorities owning 120,000 dwellings had completed LSVTs. Legislation allowing LSVTs was enacted by the 1985 Housing Act, but it was not until the 1988 Housing Act (which introduced the housing action trusts and Tenants' Choice) that local authorities gave serious consideration to transfers. The LSVTs were given a further stimulus by changes in 1989 to capital control rules, which turned LSVTs into a source of finance for 'catch-up' housing repairs. However, the response to both LSVTs and the housing action trusts was initially disappointing for the government (Audit Commission, 1993).

With LSVTs, central government assumes the role of regulator and requires local authorities to make transfers according to rules which require tenant consent. Once any outstanding housing debts have been covered, central government takes 20 per cent of the remaining proceeds of the transfer transaction. Local authorities tended to gain when interest rates were high, but in a low-interest-rate environment the financial advantages were much less clear. Often, local authorities have to increase the amount paid out in housing benefit following a transfer to the private sector, involving a rise in rents for tenants. The rents rise because the new landlords have to finance the purchase of the properties and the cost of any necessary repairs (Audit Commission, 1993).

The government claimed that transfers would enable new social housing to be created. The seventeen housing associations formed by March 1992 built over 2,200 new dwellings in 1991–92. These were mainly financed from the usable receipts from the transfer process. This represented but a tiny fraction of the total public housing stock. The situation at the end of 1993 was one that saw increasing financial constraints on housing associations and the Housing Corporation. The 1993 Budget held the prospect that financial constraints would restrict the ability of housing associations to maintain their existing capital programmes. New-build schemes would have to be financed from a steadily declining pool of resources which would place further upward pressure on rents.

An evaluation of the voluntary housing transfers using the criteria of success described in the Council Tenant's Charter reveals further problems. The Charter valued community management. It was implicit in government policy that this was especially important in urban areas afflicted by the worst social problems or where Labour councils resisted tenant empowerment. However, most of the transfers have been in smaller southern shire districts; hardly the hard-core of Labour Party municipal housing. The larger Labour-controlled authorities have been reluctant to dispose of their estates, especially when the financial advantages have become less obvious. Tenants have often been reluctant to take a chance in changing landlords, especially if there is a prospect of higher rents.

The completion of the first twenty-three transfers marked completion of the government's first round of disposals, with further applications being submitted by March 1993. The later applications were under new rules, whereby the government was keen to secure a diversity of landlords in transfer programmes. A simple handover to one large landlord could leave the market primed for a future local authority take back. The 'levy' imposed by the government on sales in the second round reflected the government's desire to offset the cost of the transfer process and reduce its impact on public expenditure (Audit Commission, 1993).

In the event, the government allowed thirteen authorities to go ahead with proposals to transfer 43,000 dwellings to housing associations in 1993–94. This was higher than originally intended since the new rules appear to have made the transfers attractive to the Exchequer, even after taking account of the necessary alterations to housing benefits (Audit Commission, 1993). Eleven of the proposed transfers involved deals with single housing associations. In these, tenants were to be asked for their consent in line with the provisions of the Council Tenant's Charter. In essence, the DoE was keen to move on with transfers because they were cost effective, even though tenants ended up paying (through increased rents) for the privilege of consenting to the changes. In this way, the rights of tenants enshrined in the Tenant's Charter were realized at a cost to the tenants themselves.

Housing action trusts

By the late 1980s, the Estate Action programme was the main method of government support for improving badly run-down local authority estates. Despite the evident value of the programme as a way of putting central government money into housing estate improvement, more needed to be done. The 1988 Housing Act provided the government with powers to establish housing action trusts (HATs) where a proposal was forthcoming from a local authority for a trust to be formed. The HATs were designed as non-departmental bodies to take over and manage major concentrations of run-down local authority housing. They were intended for areas where there were related problems concerning physical, social, economic and environmental problems that were beyond the capacity of a local authority to tackle.

The HATs were given a number of statutory objects. They were empowered to improve the condition and management of the housing on designated estates and also to become involved in a wider range of initiatives to promote regeneration. They were expected to address the economic problems of estates by assisting in the provision of local training and job creation (DoE, 1993b). In their initial form, HATs would have led to the permanent removal of estates from local authority control. This was changed later so that the local authorities could envisage the return of the estates to their control should there be local support for such an option.

Section 61 of the 1988 Housing Act prevented an order being made to establish a HAT if the majority of tenants voting in a ballot were opposed to the idea. By the end of November 1993 there were still only five HATs in existence: in Hull, Birmingham, Liverpool, Waltham Forest (London) and Tower Hamlets (London). In each case, the government consulted with tenants prior to the ballots taking place. However, critics pointed to the appointment of prospective chairpersons for the HATs before the ballots as a way of putting pressure on tenants to go along with what looked like a foregone conclusion. For example, on the Stonebridge Estate in Brent in 1993, the government appointed Tony Wade as chairman of the trust before the ballot in the area. His brief was to consult with tenants during the run-up to the vote and 'help prepare for the major tasks which the HAT will undertake' (DoE, 1993a). The presumption that HATs would definitely undertake such a role in the future reflected the kind of slant that the DoE presented to tenants before such votes.

Apart from the political suspicions of some local authorities, the HATs were constrained by the lack of resources provided by the DoE for the expansion (DoE, 1993b). New proposals for HATs were treated by the DoE on a selective basis. Reference was made to a set of criteria concentrating on the physical decline of the estates and the numbers of empty dwellings. Consideration was given to the potential for 'self-sustaining development' and the magnitude of the problems faced (DoE, 1993b).

Leasehold reform

The DoE also became aware of the need to extend the focus of the Citizen's Charter to tenants in the private sector. The occasion for this was the implementation of the government's legislation on leasehold reform. The rights of private tenants derived from similar principles to those applied in the public sector.[1]

The 1993 Leasehold Reform, Housing and Urban Development Act comprises 188 sections and 22 schedules introducing new rights and obligations affecting tenants and landlords. The provisions concern the collective enfranchisement of tenants in flats and the individual rights of tenants of flats to acquire a new lease. The Act changes the enfranchisement under the 1987 Leasehold Reform Act and covers estate management schemes in connection with enfranchisement (Williams, 1994).

The provisions in sections 1 to 38 and various schedules of the Act give long leaseholders paying a low rent in a mainly residential building the right to buy collectively the freehold of the building at market value. This right to collective enfranchisement is dependent upon a variety of factors. For instance, there is the requirement that not less than one half of the qualifying tenants by whom notice is given must satisfy a long lease residence condition. Also, the qualifying tenants must hold not less than two-thirds of the total number of flats contained in the premises.

Westminster tarnishes the image

The enfranchisement of private tenants and the empowerment of public sector tenants should have provided the Conservatives with a significant political bonus. Both kinds of tenant would benefit. This was especially the case in areas such as Westminster in central London where council tenants were keen to buy their homes and tenants under private landlords were desirous of taking advantage of collective enfranchisement and renegotiated leases.

The political impression given by the Major government's housing strategy was, however, very different in practice. In January 1994, official criticisms were made of Westminster City Council, which had been one of the Thatcher government's 'flagship' local authorities. The district auditor, John Magill, claimed that Conservative-controlled Westminster had manipulated its housing policy in an attempt to win votes for the Conservative Party. He alleged that £21.25 million had been wasted and that six councillors and four council officials might be required to repay the money. Dame Shirley Porter, who had been leader of the council until 1991, was among those named by Mr Magill (Authers et al., 1994).

The district auditor asserted that Westminster City Council had been guilty of 'gerrymandering' in favour of the ruling Conservative group on the council. The council allowed flats to remain vacant so that whole blocks could eventually be sold to owner-occupiers, who were more likely to vote Conservative than council tenants or homeless families. The council had, it was claimed, spent money on papers discussing the promotion of the Conservative's electoral interests. The sale of homes cost the council £21.25 million, including £2 million spent on placing homeless families in temporary accommodation. The empty council homes could have been used to house these families. The council lost £13.3 million by selling properties below market value.

The auditor's report created a political storm, with the Labour Party drawing attention to allegedly similar practices in other Conservative-controlled local authorities, most notably in the London boroughs of Brent and Wandsworth. For Labour, the Westminster case was symptomatic of the consequences of privatization and its linking to Tory political aspirations. In this process, it seemed that extolling the rights of tenants had sometimes been used as a convenient means to bolster the political fortunes of the Conservative Party.

Conclusions

The Citizen's Charter approach to housing represented a statement by the Conservatives that they were serious about marketizing social housing in Britain. The strategy depended upon the popular support of tenants, which was not always forthcoming. It also depended upon the willingness of local authorities to eventually come to terms with the inevitability of privatism.

However, the rights and obligations of tenants were perceived by government policy-makers only in narrow terms. The legitimate sphere of community activism was one that was instigated by way of a top-down process of estate management and the transfer of the ownership of estates to the private sector. Tenants who bought their homes during the Thatcher years found themselves, by 1990, up against the hostile conditions of a depressed property market. The impression of empowerment through home ownership was tempered by the property slump and the uncertainties of the ever fluctuating mortgage interest rate.

The political ramifications of the kind of practices disclosed by the district auditor in Westminster undermined the public euphoria of the 1980s. The right to buy had, by the mid-1990s, taken on an altogether different set of associations. Alleged local authority corruption, the 'buying' of votes through housing sales and the problems faced by the homeless were the stuff of media headlines. The desire of the New Right to replace the collectivist failed utopia with a new vision of empowerment through the market was thus severely tarnished by the mid-1990s.

Note

1. Discussion with official in the Department of the Environment, 1993.

References

Audit Commission (1993), *Who Wins? Voluntary Housing Transfers*, Occasional Papers Series, no. 20, October, HMSO, London

Authers, John, Brown, Kevin and Marsh, Peter (1994), 'Flagship Tory Council Sold Homes for Votes, Auditor Says', *Financial Times*, 14 January.

Coleman, Alice (1985), *Utopia on Trial: Vision and Reality in Planned Housing*, Hilary Shipman, London.

Department of the Environment (1992), *The Council Tenant's Charter*, DoE, London.

Department of the Environment (1993a), 'HAT Ballot for Brent Housing Estate', *Department of the Environment News Release*, no. 725, 3 November, DoE, London.

Department of the Environment (1993b), *Estate Action: New Life for Local Authorities on Estate Action and Housing Action Trusts and Links with Related Programmes*, DoE, London.

Friedman, Milton and Friedman, Rose (1980), *Free to Choose: A Personal Statement*, Penguin, Harmondsworth.

Gould, Brian (1988), *A Future for Socialism*, Jonathan Cape, London.

Jacobs, Brian D. (1992), *Fractured Cities: Capitalism, Community and Empowerment in Britain and America*, Routledge, London and New York.

Jacobs, Brian D. (1993), 'The New Right, Housing and Urban Renewal in Britain and the United States', in Jordan, G. and Ashford, N. (eds), *Public Policy and the Impact of the New Right*, Pinter Publishers, London and New York.

Lovrich, N.P. and Neiman, M. (1984), *Public Choice Theory in Public Administration: An Annotated Bibliography*, Garland Publishing, New York.

Mead, Lawrence (1986), *Beyond Entitlement*, Free Press, New York.

Murray, Charles (1984), *Losing Ground*, Basic Books, New York.

Murray, Charles (1990), *The Emerging British Underclass*, Choice in Welfare Series no. 2, Institute of Economic Affairs, London.

Podhoretz, Norman (1979), *Breaking Ranks*, Harper and Row, New York.

Slavid, Ruth (1994), 'Sheffield Plans Joint Venture with Private Firm to Run Design and Building Services', *The Architects' Journal*, 9 January, p. 7.

Williams, Del (1994), 'Leasehold Reform, Housing and Urban Development Act 1993', *Estates Gazette*, no. 9402, 15 January, pp. 100–103.

10 The Citizen's Charter and British Rail

PETER CURWEN

Introduction

The Passenger's Charter was one of the initial batch of charters in relation to which the Citizen's Charter as a whole is likely to be judged. In fact, it is probably fair to say that it is one of the three most important charters since it impinges so directly upon the daily lives of huge numbers of citizens, although it is unlikely to be perceived as of equal importance to either the Patient's Charter or the Parent's Charter.

The Passenger's Charter is unusual in one particular respect, namely its commitment to pay financial recompense to those adversely affected by trains delayed beyond specified limits. The author has had cause to avail himself of that provision but, as will be discussed below, it invites a healthy dose of cynicism which has, in many ways, served only to bring this particular charter into disrepute.

The Passenger's Charter

As with all charters, the central matter of interest to the citizen is what it says about the quality of the service that is to be provided, and especially the time lags involved before recompense is forthcoming.

The Charter opens with a bout of breast-beating (p. 4) when it declares that 'some of [these standards] are below the level you expect – and below the standards we want to achieve'. It goes on to explain that standards are set not simply for the system as a whole, but for InterCity, Regional Railways and Network SouthEast. These are set out in Figure 10.1.

Two things are immediately apparent. First, the punctuality standards are defined in terms of the scheduled arrival at the end of the route, which leaves enormous leeway to 'move the goalposts' by altering the schedule. Secondly, nothing at all is said about the other 10 per cent of trains.

InterCity

Punctuality: 90% of trains (Mondays–Saturdays, measured at the end of the route) to arrive within ten minutes of scheduled time.

Reliability: 99% of services to run.

Regional Railways

Punctuality: On long-distance routes, 90% of trains (as above) to arrive within ten minutes of scheduled time.
On short-distance routes, 90% of trains (as above) to arrive within five minutes of scheduled time.

Reliability: 99% of services to run.

Network SouthEast

Peak Punctuality (% of trains arriving within 5 minutes of the scheduled times):

90: Great Northern, Northampton Line; 89: Thameslink; 88: Chiltern South Western Lines, Kent Link, South London Lines, West Anglia; 86: Great Eastern, Solent & Wessex; 85: North London Lines; 83: Sussex Coast; 82: Kent Coast; 80: Thames, London Tilbury & Southend.

Reliability (% of trains run on weekdays):

99: Great Northern, Northampton Line, Thameslink, Chiltern, Great Eastern, Sussex Coast; 98: South Western Lines, Thameslink, West Anglia, Solent & Wessex, Kent Coast, Thames; 97: South London Lines, North London Lines, London Tilbury & Southend;

(Source: British Railways Board, 1992)

Figure 10.1   Performance standards

The Charter goes on to set out the structure of recompense where a train is delayed or cancelled 'as a result of failure on our part' (p. 14). What this means is left somewhat unclear, although 'acts of vandalism or terrorism' are specified as outside BR's control (p. 15). However, 'each claim will be treated on its merits'. Normally, the recompense will either be in the form of a voucher worth 20 per cent or more of the price paid for a journey where the delay is in excess of an hour on any leg of that journey, or an immediate refund if the train is delayed or cancelled before setting off and the citizen decides not to travel.

Passengers holding monthly and longer season tickets are offered recompense only when they renew their tickets. This comes in the form of a discount as follows:

- 5 per cent if on average over the previous 12 months *either* punctuality has been more than 3 percentage points below target *or* reliability has been more than 1 percentage point below target.
- 10 per cent if both punctuality and reliability were below the above thresholds.

To claim the discount, a new ticket must be bought within four weeks of the expiry of the old one, and must be for the same journey and for a period that is the same or shorter. BR promises to acknowledge all claims within ten working days and to reply in full within one month. Passengers who remain dissatisfied can contact one of the independent Transport Users' Consultative Committees.

The Charter concludes with the following stirring words:

> We run the rail service for you, the passenger.
> We know you want us to do better: we know we can do better – and we will.
> Care for our passengers is our prime concern: we intend to prove it.

Implementing the Charter

The business of British Rail is rather straightforward, and the expectations of citizens are accordingly clear-cut. They want trains to run regularly and to run on time. In other words, they want security in satisfying their transport needs, especially since the motor car, despite being increasingly the preferred mode of transport, has become unreliable in getting citizens to their destinations on time due to the enormous surge in the number of vehicles on the road.

On the face of it, reliability and punctuality should be easy objectives to satisfy. Mussolini, after all, was famous primarily for his ability to make the trains run on time even in Italy, and the Japanese railways are equally famous for their high-speed, reliable services. Nevertheless, this is not the view taken by British Rail itself, which is hardly surprising given its long-standing reputation as a source of repartee among strangers second only to the weather. Indeed, it is the combination of the two, epitomized by announcements that rail services have been dislocated as a result of the wrong kind of snow falling, that visitors to Britain perceive as quintessentially British.

It could be argued that BR's culture up until recently was primarily to hide behind the ramparts in the face of the barrage of adverse criticism. For example, the standard tactic when a train ground to a halt in the middle of nowhere was to tell the passengers absolutely nothing. Insofar that silence was not an option in preparing its Charter, BR's initial view was that they were being expected to deliver an assured quality of service in the face of adverse factors, such as the weather, not directly under their control.

To some extent the service quality could be improved by having much greater built-in redundancy; for example: fully staffed trains held in reserve to cover for breakdowns. Fairly obviously, however, such measures cost money, and as a nationalized industry BR was expected to keep within strictly defined spending limits. The 1980s were a period characterized by a desire on the part of government to curb subsidies, of which BR was one of the largest recipients. They were also a period characterized by a move from trains to cars, with a consequent downwards pressure upon BR's revenues. Finally, a combination of greater safety consciousness and inadequate long-term maintenance made it essential to divert resources to accident prevention.

In essence, what this suggested to BR was that if they set standards to meet citizens' highest expectations they would surely fail to achieve them, bringing down further opprobrium upon their heads. Their preference was accordingly to set targets that were conservative but just sufficiently rigorous to mute criticism. This balancing act also needed to take into account the fact that any failure to meet prescribed standards would trigger some kind of recompense.

For obvious reasons, BR shied away from recompense in the form of money as such. Not merely would it be extremely expensive but it would probably trigger a barrage of claims, each of which would have to be individually investigated at great cost in terms of staff time. Much to be preferred was a system of vouchers which would only entitle the recipient to a discount on a future journey. Not merely would this provide an incentive for the recipient to take a further journey by train, but it would be relatively cheap since it would discourage citizens from applying for the recompense. It should be noted that this method is by no means the exclusive preserve of BR. Indeed, the airline industry has long recompensed aggrieved passengers in this way, often literally giving away free tickets. In fact, the BR system is positively miserly in many respects, bearing in mind that the consequences of a delayed journey are not simply lost time but often missed appointments pertaining either to business or pleasure, which impose real costs upon the affected citizen.

Making managers responsible

Traditionally, the idea that managers should be held personally responsible for failure to meet service quality targets was alien to the culture of public enterprise. Excellent performance would elicit no obvious rewards but failure would be punished – hence no manager would be willing either to embark upon a risky course of action or to admit responsibility when things went wrong. Rather, 'it was the wrong sort of snow, guv'.

The standard procedure in the private sector to overcome this deficiency is to set tough but achievable targets, and to reward managers who achieve them. Among these targets are normally some relating to quality of service since, in theory at least, the customer is king. This suggests that where a charter applies to what is manifestly a business and one which could operate as such within the private sector (as BR may eventually be obliged to do), it ought to contain a risk/reward system comparable to private sector equivalents.

In the case of BR a certain amount of progress has been made in this respect insofar that the specification of service quality targets provides a yardstick for performance. However, very few employees are rewarded specifically as a consequence of meeting these targets, and as the targets can be flexed to make life easier for managers, they clearly leave a lot to be desired as part of a reward system for employees.

Reporting progress

According to the Second report on the Citizen's Charter (Cabinet Office, 1994, p. 22), six Network SouthEast performance targets were raised in 1993. Despite this, on average, on Network SouthEast:

- 11 out of 15 lines were more punctual;
- 10 lines were more reliable;
- 12 of the 15 achieved their punctuality targets;
- 12 achieved their reliability targets;

Further, six out of seven InterCity routes performed better than in 1992. Such success did not, however, apparently come cheap since in 1992–93 BR paid nearly £2m in compensation to passengers and forecast that in 1993–94, the first full year of the scheme's operation, it expected to pay between £5m and £6m. This increase was to reflect the fact that season ticket discounts first became available in January 1993 and the extension of the policy of inviting claims for major delays by handing out claim forms on trains.

The database provided on punctuality for Network SouthEast (p. 24) covered targets and performances for 1992 and 1993, and targets for 1994. It was notable that only one line exceeded 95 per cent in either year and that five lines did not exceed 90 per cent in either year of which one, Thames, failed to reach 85 per cent in either year and another, Kent Coast, failed to exceed 80 per cent. Despite this, the Kent Coast target was left at its habitual 82 per cent for 1994. Oh happy commuters, at least they now *knew officially* that they were going to be late one day a week. Finally, it may be noted that in only three cases, Kent Link, Kent Coast and Thames, were 1994 targets set below the level achieved in 1993. So much for aspirations!

With respect to reliability, the picture was somewhat better, with most lines achieving at least 98 per cent reliability in 1992 and 1993. The failure of 3 per cent of North London trains to run in both years was accordingly a notable feature. Do they have different snow, one wonders?

The InterCity target of 90 per cent punctuality might not strike citizens as overly taxing. It nevertheless defeated five of the seven lines in both years, and was exceeded only by the Gatwick Express in both years. The message would seem to be (if only I had heeded it!): if in doubt, catch an earlier train. Interestingly, the Gatwick Express was the only line not to achieve its target 98 per cent reliability in both years.

On the Regional Railways, 22 of the 31 groups of lines achieved their punctuality targets (see Figure 10.1) in 1993, and 13 achieved their reliability target. This rather dismal performance was recorded without comment.

An independent survey by ICM Research in March/April 1993 (see *Financial Times*, 26 August 1993) cited the balance of respondents thinking that a service had improved or deteriorated over the last year. Of the 31 services assessed, British Rail came 30th with a deterioration of 20 per cent. No doubt most of the sample questioned were commuters on the North London and Kent Coast lines!

At the same time, BR announced that potential investors in companies to be privatized should not rely upon punctuality and reliability information provided under the Charter. Although the information was independently audited by the University of Sheffield, the nature of the Financial Services Act was such that BR felt obliged to print disclaimers on station notice boards and on documentation sent out to prospective bidders.

Conclusion

As previously noted, the nature of the punctuality targets is such as to permit 'moving the goalposts'. In February 1995, it was reported by the Central Rail Users' Consultative Committee that BR had extended journey times in its timetables, normally by extending the allowance between a train's last advertised stop and the terminal station. This latter point is important because it implies no variation in the allowance between the point of departure and the last advertised stop. Hence, for example, trains between Poole and York are allowed 10 minutes to travel from Poole to Bournemouth but 19 minutes to travel from Bournemouth to Poole. It is difficult to interpret this as anything other than a device to prevent trains arriving late at Poole.

As the survey cited above indicates, citizens are not getting the message that BR's standards are improving. On the plus side they have now learnt that snow comes in different varieties, and that BR is impotent when faced by the wrong kind, not to mention by unforeseen eventualities such as leaves on the line in autumn. They may also be entitled to a voucher entitling them to a discount off their next trip, but this is not designed to improve their sense of security.

The bottom line is that BR has one enormous element in its favour: the roads are in ever-increasing gridlock. In the survey cited, the only service rated below BR was local roads, with motorways not far above. You may not get there on time with BR, but quite possibly, to cite Mrs Thatcher's immortal phrase, there is no alternative.

References and further reading

British Railways Board (1992), *The Passenger's Charter*, British Railways Board, London.

British Railways Board (1992), *BR Launches Passenger's Charter*, British Railways Board, London.

Cabinet Office (1994), *The Citizen's Charter: Second Report*, Cm 2540, HMSO, London.

Cabinet Office (1995), *The Citizen's Charter: The Facts and Figures. A Report to Mark Four Years of the Charter Programme*, Cm 2970, HMSO, London.

Doern, G. B. (1993), 'The UK Citizen's Charter: Origins and Implementation in Three Agencies', *Policy and Politics*, vol. 21, no. 1, pp. 17–19.

House of Commons Transport Committee (1995), *Railway Finances*, vol. 1, HC 206-I. Session 1994–95, HMSO, London.

11 The Citizen's Charter in Local Government

NEIL BARNETT AND SHIRLEY HARRISON

> Local authorities have historically seen the direct provision of services to the community as one of their major tasks. However, we believe that now is the time for a new approach. The real task for local authorities lies in *setting priorities, determining the standards of service which their citizens should enjoy, and finding the best ways to meet them* (Cabinet Office, 1991, p. 34, emphasis added).

This is how the Citizen's Charter introduced its section on local authorities. The implication is clear: the new approach will assign to local authorities a new role of setting and defining standards of service rather than actually providing them. The Charter identified several means by which public services were to be improved, including competition, contracting-out, performance-related pay, the use of independent inspectorates, publication of performance targets, public information on standards, complaints procedures and redress. Local authorities were encouraged, although not required, to compete for Charter Mark awards for the services they provide.

However, many of these practices were already established in local government in 1991, introduced either as a result of the government's legislative programme or voluntarily by councils responding to a changing social, economic and political environment. In some authorities, standard setting and performance measurement had been in place for years. The Citizen's Charter emerged in 1991 into a local government world much changed following a decade of intensive reform and organizational change.

Some local government initiatives pre-1991

The start of John Major's premiership found a considerable diversity within local government in terms of the political and organizational responses made during the 1980s. Many councils had adopted practices that were in tune with the Charter and many more had gone well beyond its remit. If a criticism of the Charter is that it is not really concerned with *citizenship* but rather with *consumerism*, a wide range of responses could be found in pre-1991 local government practice, which showed concern for both. As Henkel (1992, p. 84) states, however, there is 'a long acknowledged tension between the drive to integrate differences in the interests of action and to disintegrate in the interests of democracy'. It may be that the Charter adds to the means by which this equation has been progressively settled in favour of 'integration' and control by the centre.

Early in 1984 the National Consumer Council (NCC) set out to conduct a study on the measurement of local government performance, selecting the Metropolitan District of Newcastle upon Tyne and the County of Cambridgeshire as two practical examples. The NCC's choice of authorities was guided by the councils' demonstrable sympathy with the concept of the ratepayer as consumer, and their own commitment to measuring performance against standards.

> Newcastle . . . had undertaken extensive survey work among consumers . . . and the council had established an all-party Performance Review and Efficiency Sub-Committee which conducts virtually all its business in public . . . Cambridgeshire, on the other hand, had a reputation for employing modern corporate management techniques that included performance review and evaluation, and the authority had made definite efforts to communicate with the public . . . (NCC, 1986, p. vi)

These two authorities may have provided examples of good practice, but they were by no means alone. Newcastle was said to be 'at the forefront of that growing bank of authorities concerned to seek out consumers' views and feed them back into the process of political decision-making and service review' (NCC, 1986, p. xxv).

While the NCC was conducting its research in Newcastle and Cambridgeshire, the Audit Commission, the Local Government Training Board (LGTB) and the Institute for Local Government Studies were producing a handbook of good management aimed at councillors and senior officers in local authorities. It gives examples of good practice from 67 local authorities, including those engaged in the Citizen's Charter's 'real tasks' of setting priorities: 'Clwyd County Council ranks each of its activities into one of three priority bands as a means of planning the distribution of resources' (LGTB, et al., 1985, p. 29); those determining standards of service: 'The London Borough of Bexley has a well developed business process [including] a series of workload/performance targets (LGTB, et al., 1985, p. 63), and those finding the best ways to meet them: 'Berkshire County Council has developed project appraisal over a period of 10 years, resulting in greater value for money and better services' (LGTB, et al., 1985, p. 65).

Clearly, there were, even ten years ago, plenty of examples of good practice in the 'real task' of local authorities, and the LGTB encouraged local government managers to become more aware of the need to be responsive to customers by publishing *Getting Closer to the Public* in 1987. At a two-day workshop on the same theme the following year, 28 local government officers shared the experiences of authorities from all over the country, discussed achievements to date, and planned for future improvements in satisfying their customers' needs. Papers presented ranged from 'User Influence in East Sussex Social Services' to 'Better Service for the Public', in which Middlesborough explained the effect of its Putting People First (PP1) initiative. PP1 included a playground designed by the children who were going to use it.

The LGTB published *Learning from the Public* in 1988 as a guideline document for local authority managers. This explained how councils could conduct research into their customers' needs and wants and how to use the resulting information to provide better services. Twenty-three councils were quoted as good examples of this practice.

As far as performance review is concerned, the Citizen's Charter's emphasis on performance indicators is not new. A survey conducted by the Local Authorities Management Services and Computer Committee in 1980 (LAMSAC, 1982) showed that two-thirds of local authorities had some form of performance review arrangements in place. Such arrangements were encouraged and continued to flourish in the 1980s, assisted by the Audit Commission's publication of *Performance Review in Local Government* (1986) which gave a useful list of performance indicators. Thus in 1986, Pollitt could talk of 'the wave of performance assessment' which had occurred since 1979 (1986, p. 136). In 1988 the Commission published an *Action Guide*, intended as a practical manual for monitoring performance, reviewing services and taking action to improve service effectiveness. The Commission has clearly 'championed the performance review cause' (Ball and Monaghan, 1993, p. 38).

The approach during the 1980s was one of checking performance against certain standards or targets and allowing boxes to be ticked for achievement of these. The Audit Commission's *Action Guide*, for example, devotes 80 of its 101 pages to efficiency indicators and only five to indicators of service outcomes. But box-ticking without an understanding of the purpose to be served by measuring performance is at best a waste of time and can be counter-productive. If the objective of performance indicators (performance indicators) is to help authorities adapt to change, they 'need to be "tin-openers" rather than "dials" ': 'That is to say they should be indicators which help in an exploratory and interrogative process instead of providing exact answers' (Burningham, 1992, p. 95).

The response to the government's programme

Local authority management structures had altered dramatically during the 1980s as a direct result of the government's legislative programme. Competition and contracting-out had been introduced as early as 1980 in the Local Government Planning and Land Act. Compulsory Competitive Tendering (CCT) was introduced to a range of services in 1988. The purchaser/provider split was thus well established as part of local authorities' operational practice by 1991, and the Charter by itself does nothing to add to this. Further, the move towards greater internal inspection was already well in train. As early as 1981 the Department of the Environment had published a code of practice for local authority annual reports, which required them to include a prescribed list of performance indicators. Significantly, the Audit Commission had been established in 1982 to scrutinize local authorities' financial and managerial arrangements, and the remit of local authority auditors had been extended to ensuring that there were in place proper arrangements for securing economy, efficiency and effectiveness. Henkel (1992, pp. 74, 78–79) has seen the creation of the Commission as

> . . . part of government's drive to control public expenditure and to impose a disciplined, instrumental model of management on the public sector . . . the value framework within which it [the Commission] operates has more in common with central than with local government.

Further, there were knock-on effects which also inspired Charter-like responses and changes in the way authorities are managed. Services subject to competition are provided via contracts in which service levels and specifications are clearly stated. Effectively, expected standards of service are specified in advance and service delivery is monitored against these standards. There is provision for associated redress, often in the form of financial penalties upon the contractor. This has, according to Ball and Monaghan (1993, p. 36) 'led to a more performance orientated atmosphere ensuing'. Further, in the process of preparing for and operating in a new atmosphere of competition, authorities have to varying degrees sought to define customer requirements before writing service specifications, and have sought customer feedback as part of the monitoring process. A related movement has been the pursuit of quality initiatives, particularly where these are concerned with quality assurance and the definition of specific service or product standards. Beale and Pollitt (1994, p. 209), for example, point to a housing department where units operating to BS5750 standards 'had a procedures "bible" which specified standards for every aspect of their work' and which incorporated regular customer surveys. In addition, CCT has required the creation of internal trading units within councils, and standards of performance have been identified and developed for use between local authority departments.

Similar trends can be identified in other elements of the government's programme. The purchaser/provider split and the requirement to work to agreed specified standards are prominent outcomes of the NHS and Community Care Act 1990. Following the Education Act 1988, local education authorities (LEAs) now have a changed relationship with schools, offering specialist or advisory support services to both locally managed and grant maintained schools in a contractual relationship. Thus the 'enabling' authority came into being: one which was responsible for standards of service delivery but which did not necessarily deliver those services itself. The 'enabling' environment required arms-length management and the associated development of standard specifications, monitoring and feedback procedures. Other acts of parliament have incorporated the notion of standard specification and the right of users to initiate action for redress against local authorities, for example, the Environmental Protection Act 1990. In addition, the Audit Commission has, as Henkel says, 'set itself up as a source of national standards and norms against which local organizations could assess themselves and be assessed' (1992, p. 76). She claims further that the special studies published by the Commission on specific service areas (for example, the management of secondary schools in 1987) 'have laid the foundations of a national evaluative framework for local government services' (Henkel, 1992, p. 77).

Underlying these trends was the cumulative pressure on local government finance exerted throughout the 1980s and 1990s and the associated 'fiscal stress' identified by Ball and Monaghan (1993, p. 36). They point out that financial stringency forces attention to be focused on core objectives and necessitates 'difficult' decision-making.

Moving on to how councils deal with complaints and the associated area of redress, several authorities were well advanced in the implementation of such procedures. These developments are associated with the 'new' managerial concern for customer care and quality exemplified by Leicester City Council's complaints policy, which evolved into the Council's Charter (Leicester City Council, 1993, pp. 8–12). Indeed, complaints procedures were becoming a common statutory requirement and were included in the Registered Homes Act 1984, the Children Act 1989, and the NHS and Community Care Act 1990 (which also required local authorities to consult with service users). The Commission for Local Administration accelerated this trend by advising local authorities in 1989 to set up complaints procedures. Without evidence that complainants had been referred to a council's internal complaints procedure first, the Ombudsman would refuse to take up complaints.

The scope for local diversity

The cumulative effect of the legislative programme has been to enforce certain organizational reforms on to local government and to impose financial stringency. The Charter arrived in a local government world not only changed by legislation, however. As Hoggett and Hambleton (1986) pointed out, the 'old way' of organizing local government services had been criticized from two perspectives.

First, there had been *political* criticism from both the right and the left. The New Right offered a critique of perceived bureaucratic power within the public sector generally, and offered a solution based upon introducing market-based approaches. From a left-wing perspective, bureaucratic paternalism was criticized as leaving communities isolated and relatively powerless in comparison with professionally qualified officers (see, for example, Blunkett and Jackson, 1987). Both positions give rise to distinctive proposals for reform: the New Right placing emphasis upon giving greater choice and information to users of services and seeing them essentially as customers, the left taking a broader perspective and seeking to empower citizens by enhancing locally direct participative democracy, or representative democracy. Hadley and Young (1990) thus refer to the 'new right/marketeers' as attempting to promote consumer rather than producer interests in local service delivery, by the creation either of markets or market surrogates. Alternatively, they see another group of 'empowerers' concerned with the passive role of the citizen and seeking to make services more accessible, accountable and responsive. Gyford (1991) has identified the two approaches as being 'instrumental' and 'developmental'.

Secondly, again following Hoggett and Hambleton (1986), there has been a *managerialist* critique of traditional local government service delivery, driven by a group that Hadley and Young (1990) call 'organizational reformers'. This view accepts the analysis of 'inward looking' organizations developed by Peters and Waterman (1982) and paints a picture of an outdated local government management culture in the early 1980s. It is caricatured as being excessively hierarchical and bureaucratic at a time when great social, economic and technological change required a more responsive organization. Key requirements for success were to be 'closeness to the customer' or a 'customer orientation'. Flatter organizational structures were required in order to facilitate this. Prior (1995, p. 100) has thus spoken of 'the managerialist tide which flooded local government in the 1980s'. Gyford (1991) has noted that this was popular with both left and right because of its apparent apolitical nature.

The Citizen's Charter thus arrived at a time when local government had been adapting during the previous decade to organizational change, brought about by a combination of government legislation and councils' own perceptions of the need for change. Local authorities had been involved in a range of organizational reforms with a mixture of motives, aims and objectives. Concern for closeness to the customer and flatter structures had led to decentralized service delivery and attempts to delegate managerial responsibility for service delivery nearer to the point of contact with the user. A concern for giving information to the user had led to the publication of performance indicators and the development of complaints procedures and redress. Similarly, decentralization, consultation, the formation of user groups and community councils, for example, have been used as methods by the empowerers. Middlesborough had in 1985 pioneered the establishment of community and neighbourhood councils whose purpose is to:

- extend the influence of the local community over decisions made by Middlesborough Council and other bodies which affect the lives of the people living in those communities;
- provide a forum where local residents meet regularly with councillors and officers to consider matters of local importance;
- make recommendations which improve the delivery of council services;
- encourage self-help activities that involve local people in improving the quality of life and in developing community employment and other initiatives;
- control the small community budget (Shepherd, 1994, pp. 31–32).

There is clearly overlap, in that similar methods have been used for different aims. Thus, for example, decentralization can be *consumer based* and initiated out of concern for more responsive service delivery, or can be *citizen based* and concerned with the devolution of political power and increased participation.

In this picture it is difficult to determine the relevance or impact of the Citizen's Charter in local government. Elements of charterism can be found in responses based upon the political and managerial critiques of the 'old' local government. Some of the responses aimed at empowerment have gone beyond the remit of the Citizen's Charter but have incorporated elements of it. What is clear, however, is that by 1991 the scope for local diversity and experimentation was being increasingly eroded under the weight of legislation, external inspection and limitations upon local discretion over spending. As Prior points out, the Charter appeared at a time when such trends were already clear. Thus it is difficult to disentangle the influence of the Charter after 1990 from trends established well beforehand: 'for many services Charters will function more as a confirmation of, and a means of making explicit, existing processes of change rather than initiating new citizen focused developments' (Prior, 1995, p. 98).

The only significant additional requirement made of local authorities is that of being compelled to publish locally a range of annual performance indicators defined by the Audit Commission (1992). Local authorities have now undertaken the first round of publication of performance indicators and the Audit Commission has published its first national reports (Audit Commission, 1995a). The Commission undertook a consultation exercise before determining the performance indicators and is, year on year, developing and adding to them. However, doubts remain about whether differing local circumstances can be adequately conveyed by a nationally prescribed set of indicators, and about whether the indicators are too extensive and technically orientated to be of any benefit to service users interested in the quality of their service or to citizens wondering about how to exercise their vote. Most of the indicators simply replicate figures that must already be returned by local authorities to government departments or that are supplied voluntarily to the Chartered Institute of Public Finance and Accountancy (CIPFA) for the publication of their annual statistics. Many are ratios or costs per head of population, which are of little benefit without further explanation. Additionally there is concern that cost and efficiency ratios are poor surrogates for assessments of quality and effectiveness, and thus are seen as 'lop-sided' by Pollitt (1986, p. 163). He further questions who such performance measurement is for, seeing the main beneficiaries to be internal and external experts.

There is, however, scope for local authorities to provide additional information, with the Commission encouraging them

> . . . to use the local publication of their results as an opportunity to explain their reasons for particular levels of service and to publish any additional information, for example, on levels of user satisfaction, which they consider would provide a better balance (Audit Commission, 1993, p. 6).

In addition, many of the indicators allow for local performance to be shown against locally set targets (for example, telephone response times, housing repairs) and the 'contextual background' of the indicators to the public (Audit Commission, 1994b). Thus an attempt is made to explain restrictions over the ways councils run their services and how local circumstances – such as population density, social deprivation, changes in population, age of population, language, cultural and geographical differences – affect council performance. The Commission exhorts the public to 'think about the factors set out in this leaflet when you decide whether your council and other councils are giving you a good service' (1994b).

The publication of the first national reports in three volumes in March 1995, however, has not helped to allay fears. Indicators are presented council by council in the form of bar charts in descending order of score (Audit Commission, 1995b). Non-metropolitan district council results are broken down into six groups – Wales and five English regions based on amalgamations of the 'family' groups of authorities used by CIPFA for some years for comparative purposes. The information on 'contextual background' is repeated and cautionary notes are given at the beginning of the document. Thus, for example, we are told that you should not always assume that a higher figure is better than a lower one and that 'these performance indicators do not on their own give a full picture of councils' performance' (Audit Commission, 1995a, p. 8).

However, the league table approach is pursued to the full with the publication of crude bar charts signifying total expenditure per head for each authority. Despite the Audit Commission's cautionary notes it is clear that the intention is for comparisons to be made. What is not clear is what use these comparisons can be, either to citizens or to consumers of local services. There is also a danger that local authorities will divert attention to the more easily measured indicators in order to improve their league table position at the expense of the development of longer-term measures of quality or effectiveness (see Ball and Monaghan, 1993; Prior, 1995).

In addition, 1996 will see the introduction of performance indicators setting national benchmarks, which replace locally set performance targets in, for example, housing repairs and household refuse collection. The Commission has a statutory duty under the 1992 Act to facilitate comparisons between authorities and the development of an increasing number of national standards facilitates this task. The danger is that performance indicators will develop into a system in which the Audit Commission increasingly defines 'good performance' and reports where there is a 'problem'. The Commission has made it clear that it will

> . . . express a view of Local Authorities' performance as shown by the Indicators [and will] review at a national level services where Local Authorities are generally performing well and those where there appear to be problems (Audit Commission, 1995b).

The indicators do, of course, add to the amount of published information available about local authority services. Also, as the Audit Commission points out 'although Councils have the right to make local decisions, the public also has the right to see the impact of those decisions and how their Council compares with others' (Audit Commission, 1995a, p. 8).

The Audit Commission's comments on local performance have also been couched in general terms and focus on areas where 'poor' performance appears to be clearly explained by differing management practices (see, for example, the note on children with special needs in Audit Commission, 1995a, p. 11). Their tone is one of encouraging authorities to learn from good performers, rather than admonishing individual examples of poor performance. In addition it is clear that some authorities have introduced complaints procedures as a direct result of the Audit Commission's requiring information on such systems to be published as part of the performance indicators. However, in turn, it is important to set the indicators in the context of trends apparent in the external monitoring of local authorities in the 1980s and the changing relationship between central and local government.

The view of local authorities

How, then, did councils view the Citizen's Charter and its requirement for local authorities to publish performance indicators? What impact did they see it having on their 'real task'? We have seen that some councils were already well ahead of the game in 1991. York City Council is often quoted by other authorities as the pioneer, having already established its own Charters pre-1991. A survey undertaken in April-May 1995 gives some insight into the effect of the Citizen's Charter, together with a number of other initiatives, on a cross-section of authorities.[1]

A third of respondents had applied for Charter Marks for one or more of their services, with most achieving success, and half of those who had not applied saying they would be doing so in the future. The majority of respondents gave among their reasons that the award of a Charter Mark was a recognition of the high quality of their services and a natural extension to work already being done in the authority. Of those who had not applied and were not likely to do so in the future, only one gave 'political reasons' as an explanation. The majority of respondents in this category felt their own schemes, including service guarantees and quality programmes, were more meaningful, appropriate or superior to the Charter Mark scheme.

The requirement to publish performance indicators received a mixed response. The three most common responses from authorities were:

- it made us think about our accountability to the public;
- it helped us compare our performance with that of other authorities;
- it was good news for local newspapers' advertising income.

However, a significant proportion of respondents felt that comparisons with other authorities were meaningless, simply because of different ways of gathering the data.

It is noteworthy how far respondents felt that publication of performance indicators was helpful to them internally. One respondent volunteered that the exercise could be useful internally for benchmarking, while several mentioned the salutary effect it had on their staff to see their performance figures in black and white in the local paper. The effect on their external public seemed, however, to be minimal, with almost half reporting 'no feedback' from the general public since the publication of performance indicators. Of the 19 respondents who reported 'little feedback', the largest number of responses received was 44 from the local newspaper advertisement, which was incentivized. More responses were received from features or advertisements in councils' own civic newspapers than came from the paid-for advertising in the local press.

Councils were also asked about other initiatives with which they had been involved in recent years. Over 200 quality and customer care initiatives were listed, including external accreditation such as BS5750/ISO 9000, IIP and other national training awards and TQM projects. All respondents had undertaken major initiatives and many had been on-going since the mid to late 1980s. When asked about the effect of the Citizen's Charter and other initiatives, councils' own customer care and quality initiatives were seen to be most effective in helping to change and improve performance. Only one respondent said that the publication of performance indicators had great effect, and that this was patchy – only on the services where results were startling. No respondents claimed that the Charter Mark awards scheme had had great effect, not even those authorities who had successfully applied for Charter Marks and would do so again. A recurrent view of the effect of the award of Charter Marks was its publicity value.

There was no clear division along party political lines. In follow-up interviews a number of respondents identified the vision of the chief executive or the ideas of senior management as the spur to raising standards and improving performance. In some authorities, this was all part of the council's culture and ethos.

Arun District Council recognized the need to develop customer initiatives and to set standards in 1987 and adopted its chief executive's strategy *Working for the Public* in 1988. This programme had three planks: review, research and response, incorporating respectively setting standards, monitoring performance and using complaints positively to improve customer service; investigating customer needs; and responding effectively, for example in written material and by the spoken word. *Working for the Public* is a process of continuing improvement and the aims of the Citizen's Charter are

> . . . in essence our *Working for the Public* programme. The approach of the Citizen's Charter was not a new one for this authority. We were already an enabling authority. Most of our work is centred on partnerships – enabling and facilitating.[2]

Brighton Council has been researching attitudes to the council and its services since the 1980s, and acting on the results. In addition to research conducted by external contractors, regular surveys are carried out through the council's own newspaper, which bring 1,000 responses on average. Such surveys ask the public for their views on, for example, how resources should be allocated to different aspects of their work on the environment, and the council then sets priorities according to user needs.

> The service user has gained because the council has changed in that it talks to its users, but this cannot be laid at the door of the Citizen's Charter. The Citizen's Charter as a concept didn't really impinge on management because we were ahead of the things in it. Mind you, getting a Charter Mark for bereavement services was good PR and good for morale.[3]

A metropolitan district council which also has a well established research section and has been doing consumer surveys regularly saw the Citizen's Charter as

> . . . peripheral. The Citizen's Charter was not a new approach for the metropolitan districts at all. Setting priorities and determining standards of service have always been very much at the heart of what we are doing. We are taking this further and further as time goes on, well ahead of Citizen's Charter initiatives.[4]

The survey showed that the advent of CCT has without doubt made a difference to councils' practices. In response to the question on quality and customer care initiatives, the services which were subject to CCT were mentioned over and over again: leisure, cleansing, parks and gardens, vehicles' maintenance, and contract services. Generally such departments had been awarded BS or ISO accreditation. But equally there were references to personnel, finance, reception staff, social services, IT, business planning and 'whole authority' or 'across all services'.

When asked what kinds of changes authorities have faced since 1990, most replied that there had been significant reorganization of functions and restructuring or de-layering of management, with a change in organizational culture reflecting an increased focus on performance. They had been involved in business planning and the creation of business units, they had adopted an external, customer-led focus and a quarter had experienced a change of political control (pre-May 1995). Perhaps in the light of this upheaval, together with budget-slashing and major redundancy programmes, it is not so surprising that 79 per cent of respondents saw the Citizen's Charter as having no effect.

Conclusion

It may be, then, that the net effect of the Charter is to codify trends already well established, and that, as Prior points out: 'Charters can be read as public symbols portraying the particular management approach adopted by the local authority in discharging its service responsibilities to its various users' (Prior, 1995, p. 100). There is a clear danger, however, that charters simply develop into a further centralizing trend and, with the development of national standards, they become an additional means of exercising control over local discretion. We have noted the pressures for change brought upon local government by the government's legislative programme and the 'fiscal stress' of stringent financial control. The emphasis has been upon moving local service provision towards the vision of the marketeers and the Charter movement is generally consistent with these trends in that it emphasizes the need for customer information. As we have already mentioned, there has been considerable variation among local authorities in their reactions to the changing environment of the 1980s. Elements of charterism have been adopted from a variety of motives, although as Beale and Pollitt (1994) point out, these elements have been more applicable to some services than others. However, there have been strong centralizing trends imposed by legislation and, in particular, by a system of local authority finance that effectively caps the expenditure of every local authority and leaves councils to raise only 15 per cent of their expenditure locally.

From the evidence following the first publication, nationally, of performance indicators it is too early to say whether or not this diversity has been eroded any further by the Charter. It appears that the Charter continues to reflect trends already in train – to follow rather than to lead good practice. It is clear that the indicators will add to the 'national evaluative framework' identified by Henkel and that they will be used, along with earlier advice and special reports, to reinforce 'government aims to reassert a sense of central authority in the public sector' (Henkel, 1992, pp. 77, 78).

The danger is that charters develop in local government in a way that simply adds to the list of means by which local discretion and variety are cumulatively eroded. At present they appear to be of little benefit either to consumers or to citizens, but merely to be a means by which managerial control is further exercised by the centre.

Notes

1. Preliminary results from a survey of 86 local authorities (6 London boroughs, 8 metropolitan district councils, 8 county councils and 64 district councils), conducted in April 1985 and supported by funding from Leeds Metropolitan University. The 34 responses covered all types of council and divided politically into 15 Labour, 11 no overall control, 5 Conservative, 1 Liberal Democrat and 2 other. Following preliminary analysis of the data, in-depth personal interviews were conducted with a smaller sample of respondents.
2. Interview with J. Ball, Head of the Chief Executive's Unit, Arun District Council, 9 May 1995.
3. Interview with L. Greaves, Head of Communications and Marketing, Brighton District Council, 9 May 1995.
4. Interview, 10 May 1995.

References and further reading

Audit Commission (1986), *Performance Review in Local Government: A Handbook for Auditors and Local* Authorities, HMSO, London.

Audit Commission (1988), *Performance Review in Local Government: Action Guide*, HMSO, London.

Audit Commission (1992), *The Publication of Information (Standards of Performance), Direction 1992*, HMSO, London.

Audit Commission (1993), *Citizen's Charter Indicators: Charting a Course*, HMSO, London.

Audit Commission (1994a), *Citizen's Charter Indicators: Consultation on the Audit Commission's Proposals for 1995–96*, HMSO, London.

Audit Commission (1994b), *How is Your Council Performing?*, HMSO, London.

Audit Commission (1995a), *Local Authority Performance Indicators*, vols. 1, 2, 3 and Appendices, HMSO, London.

Audit Commission (1995b), *National Publication of the Local Authority Performance Indicators: Results of the Commission's Consultation Exercise*, HMSO, London.

Ball, R. and Monaghan, C. (1993), 'Performance Review: Threats and Opportunities', *Public Policy and Administration*, vol. 8, no. 3.

Beale, V. and Pollitt, C. (1994), 'Charters at the Grass Roots', *Local Government Studies*, vol. 20, no. 2, pp. 202–225.

Blunkett, D. and Jackson, K. (1987), *Democracy in Crisis: The Town Halls Respond*, Hogarth, London.

Burningham, D. (1992), 'An Overview of the Use of Performance Indicators in Local Government', in Pollitt, C. and Harrison, S. (eds), *Handbook of Public Services Management*, Blackwell, Oxford.

Cabinet Office (1991),*The Citizen's Charter: Raising the Standard*, Cm 1599, HMSO, London.

Department of the Environment (1981), *Local Authority Annual Reports*, HMSO, London.

Gyford, J. (1991), *Citizens, Consumers and Councils*, Macmillan, London.

Hadley, R. and Young, K. (1990), *Creating a Responsive Public Service*, Harvester Wheatsheaf, London.

Henkel, M. (1992), 'The Audit Commission', in Pollitt, C. and Harrison, S. (eds), *Handbook of Public Services Management*, Blackwell, Oxford.

Hoggett, P. and Hambleton, R. (1986), *The Future Rôle and Organization of Local Government (Study Paper no. 1: Emerging Patterns of Relationship Between Local Authorities and Their Communities)*, University of Birmingham, Inlogov, Birmingham.

Hoggett, P. and Hambleton, R. (eds) (1987), *Decentralization and Democracy: Localising Public Services*, University of Bristol, School of Advanced Urban Studies, Bristol.

LAMSAC (1982), *Performance Review and the Elected Member*, LAMSAC, London.

Leicester City Council (1993), 'Making complaints pay', *Industrial Relations Review and Report*, no. 546 (October).

Local Government Training Board, Audit Commission and Institute for Local Government Studies (1985), *Good Management in Local Government: Successful Practice and Action*, LGTB, Luton.

Local Government Training Board (1987), *Getting Closer to the Public*, LGTB, Luton.

Local Government Training Board (1988), *Learning from the Public*, LGTB, Luton.

Local Government Management Board (1992) *Citizens and Local Democracy: Encouraging and Managing Complaints*, LGMB, Luton.

National Consumer Council (1986), *Measuring Up Consumer Assessment of Local Authority Services: a Guideline Study*, NCC, London.

Peters, T. and Waterman, R.H. (1982), *In Search of Excellence*, Harper and Row, London.

Pollitt, C. (1986), 'Beyond the managerial model: the case for broadening performance assessment in government and the public services', *Financial Accountability and Management*, vol. 2, no. 3.

Pollitt, C. (1993), *Managerialism and the Public Services,* Blackwell, Oxford.

Prior, D. (1995), 'Citizen's Charters', in Stewart, J. and Stoker, G. (eds), *Local Government in the 1990s*, Macmillan, London.

Shepherd, C. (1994), 'Community Councils and the Citizen in Middlesborough', *Local Government Policy* Making,vol. 20, no. 4.

Wilson, D. and Game, C. (1994), *Local Government in the UK*, Macmillan, London.

Index

ANN BARHAM

accountability 29, 33–5, 52, 55–6
  and citizens' rights and duties 35–6
  and customer care 49
  in Patient's Charter 93
administration, contrast between
  management and 72, 73
anti-statism 20
Aristotle 10, 28, 29
Arnstein, S. 59
Arun District Council 150–1
Audit Commission
  establishment 142
  performance indicators: education
    108–11; local authorities 141–2,
    143, 146–9

Bachrach, P. 63
Baggott, R. 95
Ball, R. 143
Baratz, M. S. 63
Beale, V. 104, 111–12, 143
Berki, R. N. 30
Brighton Council 151
Brindle, D. 92
British Rail
  customers 46; recompense 131,
    133, 134–5, 136
  public attitudes to 134, 137
  punctuality and reliability
    standards 49, 131–2, 134, 135–7
bureaucracy, public 20, 120, 144
Burningham, D. 142
Business in the Community 119

Cambridgeshire
  local government performance 140
capitalism
  and citizenship 11–13

legitimation through customer care
  44
centralization, Charter contribution
  to 152–3
Charter 88 movement 14
Charter Mark 4–5, 149, 150, 151
charters
  and citizenship evolution 13–14
  political culture inhospitable to 14
  widespread use 1
choice
  consumers 33
  customers 31, 32
  in education 106–7, 108, 112
  and quality improvement 25, 55
citizens
  accountability to see accountability
  as clients 24, 26–7
  as consumers 74–5, 82
  as customers 19, 24, 26–7, 40–1, 74
  customers and clients distinguished
    from 27
  empowerment 59–60, 62, 64, 65,
    144–5
  limited powers of redress 58–9
  participation in public service
    provision see participation
  rights and duties see duties; rights
  state relationship with 24–5, 27,
    28–9; consumerist 50–3
  see also parents; passengers;
    patients; tenants
Citizen's Charter
  aims and objectives 2–3, 25–6,
    48–9, 55–6, 59, 72, 74, 105;
    already established in local
    authorities 139–44, 149; in
    education 102; in housing 116;

limitations 65–6;
see also specific charters
announcement 24
centralization through 152–3
and democracy 50–3
development and implementation
  4–5, 78; *see also specific charters*
impact on local authorities 142,
  146–53
individualistic emphasis 19
legitimation through 1, 17–18
as Major's 'big idea' 1, 7, 14,
  16–17
originality questioned 67
origins 2
and quality management 75, 82–3
reports on 4, 41, 136
terminology 18–19, 24–5, 27–8,
  41–2, 55–6
Thatcherite policies continued by
  17–20, 104
Citizen's Charter Unit 4
citizenship
  debate on 7–9
  and democracy 10–11
  and duties 13
  evolution 11–13; and charters
    13–14
  exclusivity 10
  extension: and capitalism 11–13
  and globalization 9
  and health care standards 89
  illusory 19
  and New Right values 15–17
  and Patient's Charter 97–9, 100
  professionalism and trust integral
    to 21–2
  rights and duties 28–9; *see also*
    rights
  skills 120
  substantive 11, 12, 13, 22
  traditional concept 9, 10–11
  undermined 7, 17–18

civil rights 12, 13, 16
civil service
  code of ethics 35
  distrust of 20
clients
  accountability to 36
  citizens as 24, 26–7
  rights and duties 30–1
Coleman, A. 120–1
collectivism
  and housing problems 119, 121
communities
  empowerment 120
  involvement in urban renewal 119
  participation in housing
    management 122–3
community councils 145–6
competition 25, 26, 45
  inapplicable to public services 51
  local authority service provision
    143
  between schools 108–9
compulsory competitive tendering
  142, 152
Connelly, J. 31, 33
Conservative Party, votes for
  and housing policy 128
constitution 8, 24
consumers 32–3
  accountability to 36
  citizens as 40–1, 74–5, 82
  customers distinguished from 31,
    57–8
  in education 111–12
  local authority responsiveness to
    140–1
  ratepayers as 140
  see also customers
corporatism 69–70
council housing *see* public housing
Council Tenant's Charter 121–4
  and housing privatization 124,
    125–6

customer care
  inappropriate in public sector 48
  legitimation through 43–4, 49–50,
    53
  local authority initiatives 150–1
  and privatization 45
customers
  accountability to 34–5, 36–7
  choice 31, 32
  citizens as 19, 24, 26–7, 32, 40–1,
    74
  consumers distinguished from 31,
    57–8
  local authority responsiveness to
    140–1, 143, 144, 145, 150–1
  private-sector role 42–4
  public housing 122
  public sector: conceptual problems
    45–7, 52, 57–8
  rights and duties 31–2
  role in determining quality and
    standards 74–7, 82–3
  satisfaction 47–8
  see also customer care

democracy
  and citizenship 10–11
  and health care 15, 51
  improvements in 52
  replaced by consumerism 50–3
Department of the Environment 118
Drucker, P. 42
duties
  citizens 28
  and rights 10, 13, 27–8
  subjects 29–30

economic recession 70
economy, state role in 68
education
  Charter impact on 102–5, 111–13
  efficiency savings 113
  government policy 103, 104,

105–7, 112, 143; promoted by
    Parent's Charter 107
  performance indicators 108–11
  political 64
  resources for 113
  see also Parent's Charter; schools
Education Reform Act (1988) 103,
    107, 143
electoral system 15
employment, full 68
empowerment
  citizens 59–60, 62, 64, 65, 144–5
  community 120
  parents 106, 111–12
  patients 93, 99
  tenants 129
  see also power
equality
  and citizenship 11–12
  see also inequality
Estate Action programme 126
Europe
  citizenship issues 8–9
  postwar reconstruction 67–70
European Convention on Human
    Rights 14
experience goods 57

fiscal crisis 17
Frankel, M. 61–2
freedom of information Acts 14
Friedman, M. and R. 119
further and higher education 103

General Will 30
gerrymandering
  Westminster City Council 128
globalization, citizenship and 9
government
  economic role 68, 70–1
  open 55, 60–5
  responsibility for enforcing health
    care standards 92

strong 71
welfare provision 68–9
see also policy-making; state
grant-maintained schools 112
Greece, ancient
  citizenship 10

Hadley, R. 145
Hambleton, R. 31, 34, 144, 145
health
  national targets 91
  rights to 96
health authorities
  responsibilities 92–3
health care
  access to: unequal 98–9
  collective responsibility for 97–8
  democratic 15, 51
  effectiveness: Charter irrelevant to
    94–6, 99–100
  priorities distorted 96, 100
  rights to 85, 87, 89–90, 100; and
    standards 88, 91
  standards 86, 88–9, 90–1;
    enforcement 91–3; limitations
    94–6
  see also National Health Service;
    Patient's Charter
Heath, Edward 117
Heater, D. 26
hegemonic project, Thatcherite
  17–18
Held, D. 9, 28
Henkel, M. 140, 142, 143, 153
high-rise housing 120–1
Hobbes, Thomas 29
Hoggett, P. 34, 144, 145
Hohfeld, W. N. 27–8
hospital waiting lists 96
housing
  leasehold reform 127
  public *see* public housing

Housing Act (1988) 124, 126
housing action trusts 126–7
housing associations 125
housing policy
  New Right 119, 121, 124–7
  Westminster City Council 128

Illich, I. 31, 34
individualism
  and citizenship 15
  emphasis on 19
  in Patient's Charter 98
inequality
  in access to health care 98–9
  increase 16
  under market-based system 51–2
information
  availability 61–4
  education in use of 64
  on educational performance 108–11
  empowerment through 60
  patients' rights to 60, 99
  unequal distribution 63
  see also performance indicators
inner cities
  regeneration: community
    involvement 119
  underclass 116–17
InterCity
  performance targets 131, 132, 136
interest groups
  policy-making role 69

Joseph, Sir Keith 117

Labour councils
  reluctance to privatize housing 125
Labour government
  NHS reforms 86–7
Labour Party
  charter proposals 2, 87
  criticism of housing privatization
    128

law enforcement
  customer concept inappropriate 46
leasehold reform 127
legitimation
  through Citizen's Charter 1, 17–18
  through customer care 43–4, 49–50,
    53
Lewis, N. 1
liberal democracy
  and citizenship 13
  role and function questioned 50
Liberal Democratic Party
  charter proposals 2, 87
liberalism 20
  see also neoliberalism; New Right
local authorities
  Charter Mark awards 149, 150, 151
  Charter principles already
    established 139–44, 149
  charters 2, 4, 149
  Citizen's Charter impact 142,
    146–53
  complaints procedures 143, 144
  'enabling' 143
  fiscal stress 143–4
  legislation on 142–4, 152
  management and organization
    140–1, 142–6, 152
  New Right attack on 15, 144–5
  obligations to tenants 121–2
  performance indicators 141–2,
    146–9, 149–50, 152–3
  priority-setting 140–1, 151
  standard-setting role 139, 143
  voluntary housing transfers 124–6
local education authorities
  performance indicators 109–11
Local Government Planning and
    Land Act (1980) 142
Local Government Training Board
    140–1
Local Management of Schools
    initiative 106, 107

Lothian Regional Council
  charter 2

MPs
  consultancy contracts 8
Magill, John 128
Major, John
  Citizen's Charter announcement 2,
    24
  Citizen's Charter as 'big idea' 1, 7,
    14, 16–17
  on family values 118
  government: education policy 104–
    5, 107; urban policy 116
  'Opportunity 2000' initiative 91
  on public service accountability 36
  underlying philosophy 104
  mentioned 4, 9
management
  administration compared with 72,
    73
  local authorities 140–1, 142–6, 152
  quality *see* quality management
  textbooks: on customers' role 42–3
managerial indicators 76
managerialism 145
managers
  British Rail: responsibility for
    performance targets 135
market
  belief in supremacy of 70–1
  customers' rights exercised through
    31–2
  inequality in 51–2
Marshall, T. H. 11–12, 22
Marx, K. 12
Matrix Churchill case 30
Mead, L. 120
medical profession
  judgement undermined 94–5
  power 86, 100
  responsibility for standards 92
Merrison Commission 97

Middlesborough
  community and neighbourhood
    councils 145–6
mixed economy 67–8, 70
mobilization of bias 63
Monaghan, C. 143
morality, public 8
Murray, C. 116–17, 119

National Consumer Council
  local government performance
    study 140
national curriculum 107
National Health Service
  democracy 15, 51
  foundation 85–6, 97
  performance targets 89, 92–3,
    94–6, 100
  power within 86–7, 100
  problems 86
  reforms 86–7
  responsibilities to patients *and*
    taxpayers 98
  values and principles 85, 97–8
  see also health care; Patient's
    Charter
nationality, citizenship and 11
natural rights 13
neighbourhood councils 145–6
neoconservatism
  critique of education 105–6
neoliberalism
  critique of education 105, 106, 107
  economic principles 70–1
Network SouthEast
  performance targets 131, 132, 136
New Right
  attitude to local authorities 15, 144
  policies: and citizenship 15–17;
    continued by Citizen's Charter
    17–20, 107; on education 103,
    105–7, 112;
    urban 116–20

values 1
  see also Thatcherism
Newcastle
  local government performance 140
Nolan Inquiry 8

Office for Public Policy 4
ombudsman 58
open government, commitment to 55,
  60–5

parents
  empowerment 106, 111–12
  rights 107–8, 111–12
Parent's Charter
  aims and objectives 107–8
  empowerment through 111–12
  impact 102–5, 111–13
  publication 102
  response to 104
  see also education; schools
Parliamentary Commissioner for
  Administration 58
participation
  and accountability 35
  encouragement 59–60; difficulties
    in 62–5
  in public housing management
    122–3
  reduction 26
  rights and duties 28
passengers
  as customers 46
  recompense 131, 133, 134–5, 136
Passenger's Charter 131–8
  see also British Rail; trains
patients
  empowerment 93, 99
  rights 88, 89–90, 100; to
    information 60, 99
Patient's Charter
  ambiguity 88, 91
  background to 85–9

and citizenship 97–9, 100
impact 94–6, 99–100
implementation 91–3
individualist emphasis 98
objectives 88, 89–91
peripheral concerns emphasized 94, 95
publication 85
Patten, John 102, 107
pay-related performance 96
performance indicators
in education 103, 108–11
limitations 57, 94–5, 103, 110–11, 142, 146–7, 148, 150
local authorities 141–2, 146–9, 149–50, 152–3
public response to 150
performance targets 48–9, 56–7
British Rail 131–2, 134, 135–7
information on 61
local authority services 143
NHS 89, 92–3, 94–6, 99–100
Peters, T. 42
Phillips, A. 22
Pirie, M. 88
pluralism 15
policy-making
corporatist 69–70
participation in *see* participation
political rights 12, 15–16
Pollitt, C. 104, 111–12, 143, 147
Porter, M. 42
power
and information dissemination 60
medical profession 86, 100
see also empowerment
Prior, D. 145, 146, 152
private sector
customers' role 42–4
public sector convergence with 72
privatization 71
central to urban policy 115–16
and customer care 45, 49

and customer choice 34
and political rights 15
public housing 123–6, 129; and gerrymandering 128
professionalism
'disabling' 31, 33–4
in education: hostility to 106, 111
and trust 21–2
see also medical profession
profitability, factors determining 43
public choice theory 20, 120
public housing
allocation 122
failure 120–1
housing action trusts for 126–7
privatization 115, 123–6, 129; and gerrymandering 128
socialist policies 123–4
public interest immunity certificates 30
public sector
convergence with private sector 72
management 72, 74
uniqueness 71–2
public services
citizen participation *see* participation
collective funding 57–8
competition: and efficiency 25, 26, 45; inapplicability 51
as experience goods 57
improvements: funding 66
information availability 61–4
no choice in use of 25–6
performance targets and monitoring *see* performance indicators; performance targets
privatization *see* privatization
standards *see* quality; standards
users redefined as customers 19, 24, 26–7, 32, 40–1, 74, *see also* clients; consumers; customers
see also particular services

public/private partnerships
  in urban renewal 115, 119
pupils, expenditure on 110

quality 25
  conceptual problems 56–7
  failure to achieve: compensation for
    see redress
  improvement: and choice 25, 55;
    funding 66
  local authority initiatives 150–1
  management *see* quality
    management
  measurement *see* performance
    indicators
  not determined by user 74–5, 82
  targets *see* performance targets;
    standards
quality management
  aims 78
  change achieved through 77–8
  Citizen's Charter provisions
    distinguished from 75, 82–3
  core elements 75–8
  implementational models 78–82

ratepayers
  as consumers 140
redress
  Charter emphasis on 3
  citizen empowerment through 64
  limitations 58–9, 65–6
  against local authorities 143, 144
  in NHS 93
  for passengers 131, 133, 134–5,
    136
refuse collection
  customer satisfaction 47–8
Regional Railways
  performance targets 131, 132, 137
rights
  citizens 28–9; and accountability
    35, 37

civil 12, 13, 16
clients 30–1
customers 31–2; and accountability
    36
  and duties 10, 13, 27–8
  evolution and extension 11–13
  guaranteed through charters 14
  to health 96
  to health care 85, 87, 89–90, 100;
    and standards 88, 91
  to information 60; on educational
    performance 108–9; on health
    care 60, 99
  parents 107–8, 111–12
  political 12, 15–16
  reduction 15–16, 17
  to school places 107–8
  social 12–13, 16, 17, 85
  subjects 29–30
  tenants 121–2, 129; private sector
    127
  see also duties
Rousseau, J.-J. 30, 79
royal prerogative 29–30, 35–6

schools
  admissions policy 108
  competition between 108–9
  efficiency savings 113
  grant-maintained 112
  league tables 108–9
  places for under-fives 110
  see also education; pupils
Scott, P. 104
search goods 57
Second World War, reconstruction
    following 67–70
sex education, rights concerning 112
shareholders 43
Sharplin, A. 42
Shepherd, C. 146
Skeffington Committee 59, 64
Social Contract 30, 79

social democracy, citizenship and 13
social rights 12–13
  health care part of 85
  reduction 16, 17
standards 25
  Charter emphasis on 3, 48–9
  in education 103, 108–11
  health care 86, 89, 90–1; and
    citizenship 89; enforcement 91–3;
    limitations 94–6; and rights 88, 91
  local authority services 139, 143,
    148, 150–1
  minimum 95
  not determined by users 74–5, 82
  and privatization 3
  train services 131–2, 134, 135–7
  see also performance targets;
    quality
state
  citizens' relationship with 24–5, 27,
    28–9; electoral democracy
    replaced with consumerism 50–3
  consumers' relationship with 33
  customers' relationship with 31–2
  subjects' relationship with 29–30
  see also government
Stowe, K. 29
subjects
  accountability to 34, 35–6
  duties and rights 29–30

targets *see* performance targets;
  standards
taxation, public services funded
  through 57–8
taxpayers
  citizens as 55
  NHS responsibilities to 98
teachers, parental support for 112–13
tenants
  activism 123
  ballots on housing action trusts
    126–7

charter 121–4, 125–6
  empowerment 129
  private sector 127
  rights 121–2, 127, 129
  self-help encouraged 122–3
  tenure, security of 122
Thatcher, Margaret
  belief in market 70
  conviction politics 18
  urban policy 116
  mentioned 87, 116
Thatcherism
  Charter as continuation of 1, 7,
    17–20, 104
  and citizenship 15–16
  education policies 105–7
  values 1–2, 7, 16
trade unions
  power reduced 15
trains
  delayed/cancelled: recompense for
    131, 133, 134–5, 136
  journey times extended 137
  punctuality and reliability standards
    131–2, 134, 135–7
trust, professionalism and 21–2

underclass 116–17
United States Supreme Court 29
urban policy 116–20
  privatization central to 115–16
  see also public housing

value
  public services 25
values
  in Citizen's Charter 3
  NHS 85, 97–8
  New Right 1, 15, 16, 17–18, 20; *see
    also* individualism; privatization
  in quality management 76–7
  Thatcherite 1–2, 7, 16
voluntary housing transfers 124–6

waiting lists, hospital 96
Waldegrave, William 4, 50, 97
Walsh, K. 50, 56, 57
Waterman, R. H. 42
welfare benefits
  and social obligations 120
welfare state
  costs 17
  cuts in 16
  dependency on 116–17, 118
  postwar consensus on 68–9
  see also health care; public housing

Westminster City Council 128
Wilson, E. 19
women
  citizenship 99

York City Council
  charter 2, 149
Young, H. 20
Young, K. 145